COLLINS GEM GUIDES

FRESH AND SALTWATER

FISH

illustration by
Keith Linsell

text by
Michael Prichard

COLLINS
London and Glasgow

This COLLINS GEM GUIDE covers marine species
of the North-east Atlantic, and freshwater
species of Britain and Western Europe.

Previous page: Roach

First published 1986

© in the illustrations Keith Linsell
© in the text Michael Prichard

ISBN 000 458827 4

Colour reproduction by Adroit Photo-Litho Ltd, Birmingham

Filmset by Ace Filmsetting Ltd, Frome, Somerset

Printed and bound by Wm Collins Sons and Co Ltd, Glasgow

Reprint 10 9 8 7 6 5 4

Contents

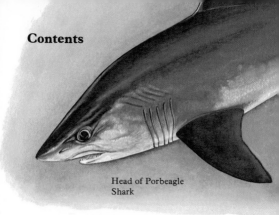

Head of Porbeagle
Shark

Introduction

What is a fish? For centuries considerable confusion existed concerning the true definition of the word. Most people thought that anything living in water had to be a fish. Others who were more observant thought that the possession of fins was a necessary qualification. However, this thinking was still wrong because it brought fish and mammals into the same group of creatures.

Fish can be simply defined as creatures that live all of their lives in water, are cold-blooded, take in oxygen from the surrounding water through gills, do not exhibit placentation and cannot suckle their young. Aquatic mammals, such as Whales and Seals, do have fins with which to move but they also have warm blood, grow their young in a uterus and suckle for a protracted period. Higher mammals also teach their juveniles family and social behaviour. There is little if any parental care by most male or female fish, although some species do build nests and guard both the eggs and hatching fry. Usually spawning is on a haphazard basis, with fish broadcasting their eggs and milt in the surrounding water. The eggs are then left to survive as best they can!

Although vertebrates, not all fish possess a bony skeleton. Some species, notably the sharks and skates, have a skeletal structure composed of gristly cartilage. They developed after the Devonian period

A meandering river will hold most freshwater species throughout its length; Trout in the headwaters and coarse, shoal fish in the slow-running stream

and must have been so well adapted to their environment as to have little need to evolve to any great extent. These groups of fish are of much older origin than the true bony fish.

There are about 20,000 species of fish spanning the fresh and saltwaters of the world. About 5000 species live in freshwater, and a few, such as Salmon, Sturgeon and Eels, move periodically between the two conditions.

How to use this book

Fish appeared on the earth millions of years ago, long before the animals, which we recognize today, existed. At that time most creatures lived in water. Some air-breathing creatures, such as the dinosaurs, needed water to support their massive bulk. Fish, although possessing rudimentary limbs, have never lived permanently on the land mass. It would seem that most fish are perfectly adapted to the medium in which they live.

The gristle fish *Selachians* arrived first, followed by two other groups of fish; the bony fish, and the lampreys and hagfish. The former group has by far the greatest number of species, living in both fresh and saltwater. Scientists will tell you that, strictly speaking, only the bony fish can be truly termed 'fish'. For purposes of identification, we will consider them all as true fish.

Geological Strata Periods

					Mammals – Birds		
Recent	Pliocene	Oligocene	Eocene	Cretaceous	Reptiles	Jurassic	Triassic
					Fish		

Dominant Creatures

Much of what we know about the early forms of fish has been learned from fossil remains. Some splendid examples exist, in natural history museums, which indicate that few changes in skeletal make-up have occurred over the passage of time.

Fish can be identified by asking a series of questions concerned with how the fish looks externally:

1. Shape of the body
2. Position and number of fins, and whether spined or soft
3. Possession of teeth and their type
4. Type of skin or scales and the number that can be counted in a defined area
5. Colour of skin or scales
6. Possession of thorns, spurs, barbules, tubercles, coloured patches, visible sexual appendages or any other noticeable characteristics

1. To make an accurate identification, first ask the question: 'Is the fish large or small?'. Then, 'Is it round, or flat?'. Establishing the shape of a particular

200 million years   400 million years

| Permian | Upper Carboniferous | Lower Carboniferous | Devonian | Silurian | Ordovician | Invertebrate Dominance → |

fish will lead to a narrowing down of the field to sensible proportions.

2. Fins are important limbs of locomotion and their number and position on the fish's body changes from one species to another. Some fish, the Cod for example, have three dorsal fins. So, seeing or catching a marine fish with that number of fins will put it into the Cod family, which narrows down the identification search.

3. All fish have teeth, but they aren't always apparent! Freshwater Carp have throat teeth called *pharyngeals* for grinding food items. They are positioned at the entrance to the Carp's gullet. Sharks have vicious teeth that can be clearly seen as

Anatomy of the **Perch**

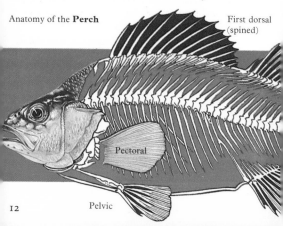

First dorsal (spined)

Pectoral

Pelvic

instruments for cutting and tearing flesh. The Whiting has a mouth full of tiny, sharp teeth intended for grasping and trapping smaller fish, on which it feeds.

4. Fish have skin into which scales are embedded. Sometimes the scales are large, soft and easily seen. These are described as being *cycloid*. There are some species that have minute scales which appear almost as smooth skin. Over the scales there is usually a coating of protective slime, acting as a barrier to water and preventing access to infection. The Sea Bass has scales that are hard, with a raised point on the rear edge. These are called *ctenoid*.

Many reference books advise you to count the number of scales along the fish's *lateral line*; this is a clearly defined line of scales along each side of the body which acts as a sensory organ, enabling the

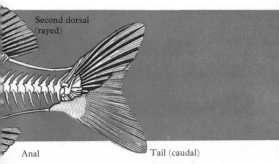

Second dorsal
(rayed)

Anal

Tail (caudal)

fish to feel vibrations and gauge its proximity to underwater obstructions. Counting scales will work admirably with fish of one species. But, in freshwater certainly, there may well be a degree of hybridization between a number of closely-related species that inhabit the same water space. Hybrids, though strongly resembling one of the parent fish, will have a peculiar scale count.

5. The colour of skin or scales cannot be used as an isolated identification point. The body colour of a fish may well depend on the colour of the environment, and whether the habitat is well lit or very dark. Rock Codling are a splendid example of fish that take on the rich, reddish hue, similar to the kelp-strewn habitat in which they live. In earlier times, the Brown Trout *Salmo trutta* was thought (because of its many colour variants) to be a number of different species, depending on where it was found. The truth is that habitat often conditions colour and, to a lesser extent, the body shape of the fish. Even fish

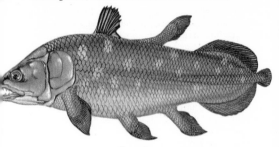

that are hardly ever confused with near relatives, such as the Tench, can produce confusing colorations.

Cuckoo Wrasse are one species in which there is a year-round difference in colour between sexes. A near relation, the Ballan Wrasse, displays a fantastic array of colourings among a collection of individuals coming from the same habitat. Both of these situations have led anglers and naturalists into thinking that they were inspecting different species, rather than species/sexual colour variants.

6. When looking at a catch of Rays some will have distinctive spots and others may have sharp thorns. The position and type of markings or thorns will give the clue to the species – the overall colour can and does alter.

Among the larger sea fish subtle external features are more easily detected. The lateral keels of the Porbeagle Shark are pronounced and make a useful

15

identification point. Spurdogs and Smoothhounds are somewhat alike until one looks closely at fins and mouths. The large, sharp spine that precedes both dorsal fins on the Spurdog give the fish its name. Inspecting the mouth and teeth can help when trying to arrive at a name. Smoothhounds are members of the same group of fish as the Spurdogs but they feed on different animals. Their teeth are of a flat, grinding kind, used to crush crabs and other small crustaceans. The small, needle-like teeth of the Spurdog are intended to grasp pelagic shoalfish as they try to escape into the upper water layers.

Sharks, Skates and Rays have visible, external differences. Male fish have a pair of elongated claspers, used when copulating. Each of these families of fish vary from the bony fish in that the females are fertilized internally.

A final identification check is to ask yourself whether a particular fish ought to be in its immediate habitat. Finding a Flounder high up in a river is not unusual, for this marine species is highly tolerant of freshwater and annually ascends into rivers to feed. However, beware of identifying it as a Plaice because of the orange spots that may be on the body. The Plaice is similar in shape but is a totally marine species that would never be found in freshwater.

Freshwater fish also have their habitat preferences. The Rudd is unlikely to be found in a fast-flowing stream, but its close relative, the Roach, which looks remarkably similar, would be far more likely to inhabit the stream.

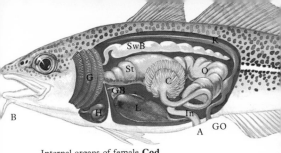

Internal organs of female **Cod**

Cod
- G – gills
- H – heart
- SwB – swim bladder
- St – stomach
- K – kidney
- O – ovary
- In – intestine
- A – anus
- GO – genital opening
- L – liver
- GB – gall bladder
- C – cloaca
- B – barbule

Spurdog
- Spn – spleen
- In – intestine
- P – pancreas
- L – liver
- H – heart
- T – testis
- K – kidney
- St – stomach
- Sp – spine

Male **Spurdog**

The freshwater environment

Water both supports the bodies of fish, and provides oxygen to sustain life, while allowing fish to move about. Water is continuously supplied as rain, or snowmelt from mountains. Oxygen is a constituent part but it can also be added by wind ruffling the surface of a pond, when water falls, such as over a weir sill, or when a tiny stream rushes down a steep gradient. Oxygen is also introduced into the water by waterplants, by a process known as photosynthesis.

Fish like clean water in which to live, feed and reproduce. Various species have different oxygen demands. Brown Trout *Salmo trutta* look for a high oxygen content, whereas Carp *Cyprinus carpio* can live in situations that offer a very low amount. Some

A still water in summer

Epilimnion (warmest)

Thermocline (band of changing-temperature water)

Hypolimnion (coldest)

fish are more tolerant than others of poor quality water but few fish can survive the serious pollution, in the form of vast amounts of man-made toxic substances and effluent from farms, which constantly pours into lakes and rivers.

Fish will select areas, in any piece of water, to suit their life style, varying their habitat by periodic moves to find food either as an individual fish or as a member of a shoal or age group. There may be seasonal migration to breed, to escape predators or to seek suitable temperatures. Juvenile fish may even wish to depart from an area that holds adults of their own species – in short, they are always looking for comfortable surroundings. Fish found in rivers display slightly different migratory behaviour to members of the same species that live in still water. Water temperature has less effect in rivers, as the heating up and cooling down processes are much slower.

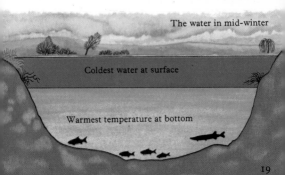

The water in mid-winter

Coldest water at surface

Warmest temperature at bottom

19

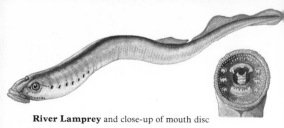

River Lamprey and close-up of mouth disc

RIVER LAMPREY *Lampetra fluviatilis*

This fish, and its associated marine species *Petromyzon marinus*, have little in common with the *Selachians* or bony fish. They are primitive vertebrates with a cartilaginous structure and an Eel-shaped body. Lampreys have no paired fins on their scaleless bodies. The jaws are the most interesting feature of the fish. Shaped as a circular disc, the River Lamprey's mouth has a single row of horny teeth while the sea species has multiple rows of teeth, used to create a holdfast on the body of another fish. The Lamprey then sucks the blood of its victim. During this feeding process, the Lamprey infiltrates a substance into the wound that stops coagulation of the blood.

Lampreys have a rudimentary gill formation. Water (from which oxygen is taken) is drawn into the mouth, or through the seven gill openings when the fish's jaws are adhered to the skin of its live meal. There are no gill cases or swim bladder. Both species spend a large part of their lives in saltwater, although

Sea Lamprey and close-up of mouth disc

they breed in the headwaters of rivers and streams. Breeding fish undergo a bodily change as they travel upriver; the dorsal fins become bigger and the fish exhibits no desire to feed.

Spawning takes place from February–June in furrows or holes, made by the male fish, on stony gravel bottoms; on completion of spawning the adult fish die. The eggs, numbering many thousands, hatch in a few weeks into blind, toothless larvae that burrow into the mud of the riverbed. After 2–5 years, they metamorphose into the true Lamprey shape and gradually make their way to the sea to grow to adult size.

Both the River and Sea Lamprey are caught in nets and wicker traps set for eels in a number of rivers in Britain and Europe. It is doubtful whether they are highly regarded as a fish for the table, particularly as King Henry I of England was said to have come to an untimely death after eating a surfeit of them!

STURGEON *Acipenser sturio*

The Sturgeon, though rarely seen, is widely known as the fish that provides us with caviar. It has another claim to fame as a 'royal' fish, for over the centuries any Sturgeons caught in British rivers were always offered to the monarch. It can grow to a huge size; one landed at Grimsby, in the last century, measured over 11 ft (3.35 m) in length and weighed 623 lb (282.6 kg).

This Northern Hemisphere fish has a number of primitive characteristics. The body is long and streamlined with five rows of hard, bonelike plates (scutes). The fish's head is also protected by a shield of scutes. Four barbules are present in a line across the underjaw. The snout is pointed, with a small mouth, behind the barbules, that can be protruded. There are no teeth, which suggests that the Sturgeon feeds by rooting around in the soft mud of the sea and riverbed for small food items. The Sturgeon has a powerful tail with a larger upper lobe. The remaining fins are quite small when compared to the size of the body.

The membrane of the swim bladder is used, commercially, to provide us with isinglass, a gelatine used in the production of confectionery and the refining of alcoholic drinks.

Although primarily a marine species, the Sturgeon will travel far up into freshwater to spawn and is often caught in Salmon nets in estuarial waters. The species provides the USSR with one of that country's most precious exports – caviar.

Sturgeon

THE SHADS

These Herring-like fishes are said to be anadromous; they live most of their lives in saltwater yet migrate into freshwater to breed, after which the parent fish return to the sea. Many eggs are shed and they usually hatch within two weeks. Juvenile fish may stay in the river for 12 months or more, before descending with the current to the sea to take up a marine life. There they feed on minute plankton, although the Twaite Shad juveniles will hunt larger fish fry.

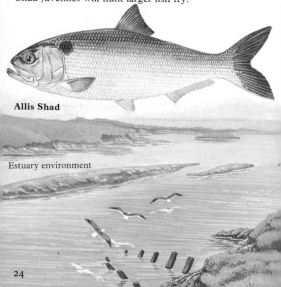

Allis Shad

Estuary environment

The **Allis Shad** *Alosa alosa* is a slender, silver fish with a dark blue back and a possible row of black spots along its flanks. The lateral line, normally visible on most round fish, is poorly represented in both Shad species. Principle distinguishing features between the two fish are the flank spots and gill rakers. The Allis Shad can have one large blotch behind the gill-case, with further paler spots behind it; the Twaite Shad has 6–10 in total. The former species has a mass of dense gill-rakers, over 100 on the first gill arch, whereas the latter has only about 50. Both fish attain a maximum weight of 3 lb (1.36 kg).

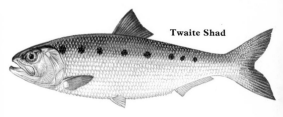

Twaite Shad

The **Twaite Shad** *Alosa fallax* has a wider distribution than its close relative. It can be found entering rivers, and offshore in places as far apart as Norway and Turkey! Neither fish has any real economic importance, although they are both trapped in estuary nets as they enter freshwater on their annual spawning migration.

ATLANTIC SALMON *Salmo salar*

The Salmon begins life in freshwater, high upstream in the headwaters of pure, cool, highly oxygenated rivers. In late autumn or early winter, the female fish constructs a 'nest', known as the *redd*. She scrapes a hollow in the gravel of a fast-flowing shallow and spawns in it. Then she covers the fertilized eggs by fanning the loose gravel with her tail. The male fish's function, apart from joining the female to ensure fertilization, is to guard against the arrival of other breeding pairs, that would rip up the earlier-spawned eggs.

The effort of travelling thousands of ocean miles to the river of their birth, coupled with the tortures of wending their way upriver, ensure that after breeding, few adult fish ever get back to the sea. For Salmon do not feed when in freshwater. They rely totally on the nourishment gained when feeding in such food-rich places as the deep water off Greenland and Iceland to get them through the rigours of breeding. Many die in the upriver pools, while a few of the stronger fish drop down on the current flow to saltwater, where they make their way back to the established feeding grounds. Known as *kelts*, they are seen by keen observers as spent, bedraggled shadows of their former proud shape.

Salmon eggs hatch in 90–130 days, depending on water temperature. The newly-emerged *alevins* feed on the sustenance provided by the yet to be absorbed yolksac. Gradually they pass through a fry development to take on the parr appearance: a richly-

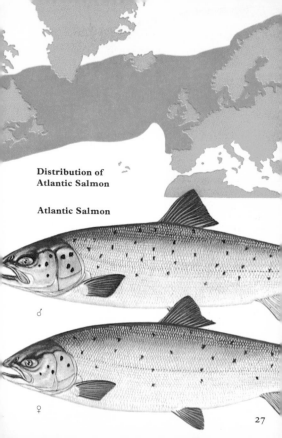

**Distribution of
Atlantic Salmon**

Atlantic Salmon

♂

♀

27

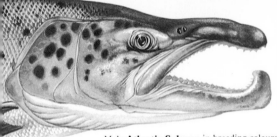

Male **Atlantic Salmon** in breeding colours, showing much-enlarged kype

coloured pelage of black back, with dark vertical bars over bright silver scales dotted with reddish spots. Salmon parr forage for plankton and grow quickly in the warming water. Some stay in freshwater for only one year; they then change their colouring, becoming silvery *smolts* and leave for the sea. Others remain for up to three years in the river. Salmon, after their rich feeding in the sea, may return to the river they were spawned in after any number of years spent growing in oceanic waters. A fish that returns after only one year is called a *grilse* and might weigh about 5 lb (2.2 kg). Fish that return after a few years could weigh as much as

Low water salmon fly (Silver Blue)

Fully dressed salmon fly (Thunder & Lightening)

The adipose fin, a fleshy appendage without rays, is to be found on members of the Salmon family

Humpback Salmon

60 lb (27.2 kg). The British Rod Caught Record is a fish of 64 lb (29 kg).

S. salar is a streamlined, powerful fish with a blue-black back, silver sides and creamy-white under-belly. In freshwater, both adult sexes change into a breeding pelage, becoming more reddish. The male fish grows a *kype*; a hooked underjaw, often so extended that the fish cannot close its mouth.

Occasionally the European side of the Atlantic shore sees the arrival of the **Humpback Salmon** *Oncorhynchus gorbuscha*, a north Pacific fish that could be encountered, as the species has been intro-duced, by the Soviets, to the rivers that spill into the White Sea. The male fish has a pronounced hump, forward of the dorsal fin, that gives it its name.

Garry tube fly   Orange shrimp fly   29

BROWN TROUT *Salmo trutta fario**

The Brown Trout is regarded as being among the best of sporting fish and enjoys a worldwide reputation for its fight and for the delicacy of its flesh at table.

Although primarily a fish of the Northern Hemisphere, man has taken the Brown Trout to a variety of habitats in many countries. Successful living and breeding depend largely on water quality. Like the Salmon, to whom it is closely related, Brown Trout are a valuable food resource and have been farmed extensively for many years.

Trout are members of the Salmon family, which means that they ought to demand water conditions of purity and high oxygenation. In reality the species is to be found in a wide variety of waters, some of

* I follow the advice of an eminent writer, and friend, Fred Buller, in establishing clarity in identification by using *Salmo trutta fario* to establish the Brown Trout. Sea Trout, although technically of the same species when discussed by ichthyologists, have a different appearance and behaviour so will be named as *Salmo trutta trutta*.

♂

doubtful water purity. Brown Trout are found in rivers and in still waters. We assume the Trout will be found in the headwaters of a highland river – and they will be there but they will also be far down in the middle, slow-running reaches. Even in estuaries, the slob Trout is often taken in nets, sufficient evidence that the fish has a toleration for salt and brackish water.

Many of the largest Trout seen come from still waters, particularly those found in limestone regions. The lime content ensures high fertility for the water, producing an abundance of water plants and invertebrates upon which the Trout feed. The Brown Trout may be considered a major predator in any water. From parr age on, much of the fish's life is spent feeding on fry of other species.

Trout can vary tremendously in coloration. The classic fish would be a rich, green-brown on the back, lightening to creamy brown flanks and yellow belly. Trout of all ages are richly spotted. Both sexes display black and red spots on the gill cases and

Winged wet fly
(Black Midge)

Hackled dry fly
(Red Tag)

body, becoming fewer towards the tail fork. The red spots have a fringing of creamy white. Trout scales are small and smooth. When handled, the fish has a soft, floppy feeling so unlike the stiff body of a fresh Salmon.

Brown Trout breed from late autumn into the first months of the following year. The female becomes mature at three years old, whereas male fish are sexually precocious a year earlier. Trout move from deep water, in rivers or lakes, to gravelly shallows in fast-flowing feeder streams, where the female fish scrapes a redd among the small stones. After fertilization, the eggs are covered by the female scraping a further depression in the gravel. With a water temperature of about 6°C, the eggs hatch in eight weeks. Young alevins then spend their time avoiding predators as they gradually absorb the yolk sac.

In their first year of life the parr adopt a similar diet to their cousins, the Salmon, eating tiny larval water insects and invertebrates. Adult Trout add the emerging nymphs and fully winged insects to their diet, behaviour that has given birth to the sport of wet and dry fly fishing; here man-made insects are tied from feathers, thread, tinsels and fur, and are fished below or actually on the surface of the river or still water. The game fisherman can hunt the Trout by simulating the fish's natural food, casting streamer flies that represent small fish, and all manner of metal and plastic spinning lures.

In all probability, more words of praise have been written about this species than any other of our freshwater fish. It deserves a fine international reputation as a fish that can outwit many of its ardent followers.

SEA TROUT *Salmo trutta trutta*

The Sea Trout (below), which is a migratory version of the Brown Trout, is second only to the Salmon in value to the inshore fishing boat and the estuary netsman. In shape, it looks like a Salmon, but with smaller silver scales giving the fish a sleek appearance. The tail is nearly squared off with no apparent fork. Small black spots cover the body above the lateral line. A clearer identification point is that the upper bone of the mouth extends beyond the fish's eye, while that of the larger Salmon ends at the rear edge of the eye.

Sea Trout enter the mainly western rivers of England and Wales, most rivers in Ireland and Scotland, and Continental rivers from the Arctic to the Bay of Biscay, to breed. They choose a similar spawning environment to the Brown Trout. It is said that the two varieties can interbreed successfully.

Sea Trout

RAINBOW TROUT *Salmo gairdneri*

Rainbow Trout

This Trout was introduced from North America and is today stocked all over Europe as an angling and fish-farming species, but does not really succeed as a wild breeding species here. It grows quickly, but is artificially spawned for a higher fecundity. They can tolerate high water temperatures, which makes them an ideal species for stocking into quite shallow lakes, where they 'rise' freely to insects that live in the water and hatch out at the surface. Small, colourful scales give the fish its name.

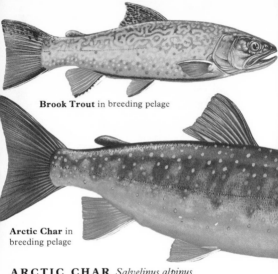

Brook Trout in breeding pelage

Arctic Char in
breeding pelage

ARCTIC CHAR *Salvelinus alpinus*

An anadromous fish of northern seas and rivers, this
Char is land-locked in British waters. Char are found
in a few of the larger waters of the Lake District, and
a number of small loughs in mountainous regions of
Ireland. They can be said to be remnant arctic
fauna, left by the retreating ice of the last ice age.
The male fish adopt a highly colourful breeding
dress after following the female fish in from the sea.
Like all members of the Salmon group, Arctic Char
make splendid eating.

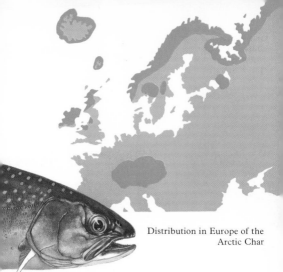

Distribution in Europe of the
Arctic Char

BROOK TROUT *Salvelinus fontinalis*

Another introduction from North America, the
Brook Trout is in fact a Char! It is readily identified
by the curling lines of light colour on the dark greenish body, giving it a marbled appearance. Brook
Trout tolerate high water temperatures, so can be
stocked into lowland fisheries, although in America
it inhabits cold highland streams. Like the Arctic
Char, it changes into a bright pelage at spawning
time which is extended through the late autumn and
early winter months.

37

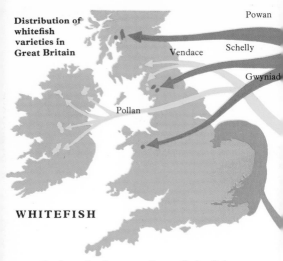

Distribution of
whitefish
varieties in
Great Britain

Powan

Schelly

Vendace

Gwyniad

Pollan

WHITEFISH

A collection of minor members of the Salmon
family, the Whitefish are all silvery, with fairly large
scales and an adipose fin. Identification is not easy
as there are similarities between species and the
taxonomists seem unable to agree upon scientific
names. The three fish, *Coregonus laveratus spp.* that
follow are thought to be derived from the **Houting**.
Powan inhabit Loch Lomond and are said to be the
main diet of that lake's legendary Pike. **Schelly** are
fish of the Lake District and the **Gwyniad**, as its
name implies, belongs to a few Welsh waters.

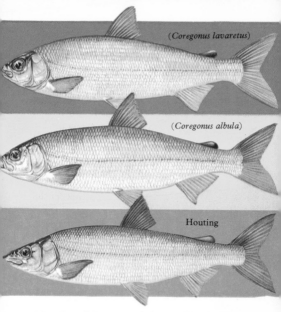

(*Coregonus lavaretus*)

(*Coregonus albula*)

Houting

(Another of the group of Coregonids, the **Vendace**, *Coregonus albula*, has its home in Loch Maben and Lough Neagh, where they are netted for food.)

One member of the group is sea-going; Houting are occasionally found in estuaries in northern Britain but is widely, though thinly, distributed in the Baltic. **All the Whitefish are declining, as a breeding stock, in European waters.**

GRAYLING *Thymallus thymallus*

One of nature's most beautiful fish, the Grayling cannot be mistaken. It is found throughout Northern Europe but only locally in Britain. The body, graceful and lean, is covered in bright silver scales with a number of horizontal purplish stripes along the flanks. The dorsal fin is unmistakable, a giant sail used to good effect in fast water to establish the fish in its chosen resting place. Grayling have a characteristic smell, like that of the garden herb thyme! The fish does not enjoy a good reputation among Trout owners, who see the fish as a competitor for the

Grayling

Smelt

available food that the higher-prized Trout could be eating. But in the ecosystem Grayling can be relied upon to hold their place by utilizing, successfully, the food available that Trout might ignore.

Unlike other members of the Salmon tribe this species spawns in the spring, depositing many eggs in a shallow redd. Close observation will show that the male fish wraps his huge dorsal fin across the female as the eggs are fertilized. The eggs hatch quicker and the fry grow much faster than the native Trout that inhabit the same environment.

SMELT *Osmerus eperlanus*

A small fish, slender in shape, with tiny defined scales and a mouth that appears too large for the body. It spawns in freshwater but lives in the sea, close inshore, feeding on the fry of other species. When freshly caught the fish smells faintly of cucumber!

PIKE *Esox lucius*

Loved by many naturalists but sometimes despised as a ruthless predator, Pike perform a vital function in freshwater. They are the 'regulators' for many still waters and rivers, ensuring that the environment does not become overcrowded or contain masses of stunted and ailing fish. But Pike only take sizable fish, whereas Trout are responsible for massive predation among the eggs and fry of most species. There is one genus and only one represented species in European waters, although *Esox* has close relatives in Asia and North America.

A freshwater food chain

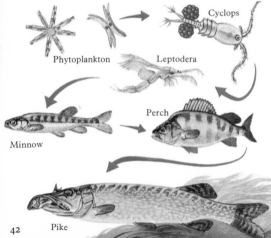

Phytoplankton

Cyclops

Leptodera

Minnow

Perch

Pike

Pike, showing camouflage

Pike are perfectly designed for ambush. Sleek and powerful, they can move very fast over short distances. The Pike is superbly camouflaged with a green-bronze body shading to a creamy-white belly. There are lighter, regular marblings of yellow on the flanks with smaller spots above the lateral line. The paired fins appear small but close observation will show that the muscled body and large tail indicate tremendous power.

43

Skull of Pike, showing dentition

The head is large, with a marked extension of the lower jaw. There are a huge number of teeth; the larger ones are for gripping prey, and the dense pattern of teeth seen on the roof of the fish's mouth are used as a one-way trap. A fish can get in but it cannot get out. The meal is grabbed crosswise, then turned and swallowed. Smaller specimens, up to 6–9 in (15–23 cm), feed on minute larvae and other water creatures found in the shallow areas of lakes or running waters. Over that length, Pike adopt a diet solely consisting of live and dead fish, amphibians, small water mammals and birds. The Pike is known to engage in acts of cannibalism; instances of a fish attempting to eat another of its own size are quite common. Pike have binocular vision, vitally necessary in a fish that has to judge the distance between itself and a possible meal.

Pike take a fish sideways, and turn it head-first before swallowing

Pike take a wide range of fish and animals, including water fowl!

Pike are among the earliest coarse fish to spawn and favour special breeding areas to which they return each year. From early February to April, particularly at times of flooding, they move to shallow areas with heavy weed growth. Each female is accompanied by a number of smaller males. **Note that all large Pike are female, the male fish rarely exceeding 10 lb (4.5 kg) in weight.** The eggs are shed among the weedfronds, where they hatch in 10–40 days, depending on the warmth of the period. The minute Pike larvae soon attach themselves, by an adhesive gland on their heads, to weed. They rest during the absorption of the yolk sac, which takes up to ten days. During this time, gill and fin development takes place. They then become free-swimming and begin feeding on plankton.

Many tales are told about 'monster Pike'; some have foundation because the Pike will grow in direct ratio to the amount of fodder fish present in its territory. This species does not have to be old to grow large. A female Pike of over 50 lb (22.7 kg) was netted from Lough Mask; aging, which can be done by reading scales or the operculum bone for annual growth rings, indicated that the fish was only just over eight years old. Loch Lomond, along with many of the other large lakes of the British Isles, is legendary for the enormous Pike that it holds.

ROACH *Rutilus rutilus*

The Roach belongs to the Carp family *Cyprinidae* which is the biggest family of fish on earth. The most widespread freshwater fish in Britain, Roach can be found in both running and still waters from the south of England up to the beginning of the Scottish Highlands. The Roach was not an indigenous species in Ireland but was introduced, as legend has it, by English Pike fishermen in the early part of this century. Since that time it has spread from the Cork Blackwater and Ulster Erne to many other connected river systems. On the Continent there are a number of allied species as well as *R. rutilus*, which seems to be confined to northern Europe, above the Alps.

Roach are brightly coloured fish. They have a rich purple-black back shading down the flanks to silver

scales ending in creamy-white underparts. The scales are fairly large and hard-edged, lacking any apparent slime until after spawning, when the fish lose their condition and colour. The fish's fins are reddish in hue, though juveniles or fish from poor quality waters have adulterated, pinkish fins. There has always been some confusion between this species and the closely related Rudd. Two simple identification points are the position of the dorsal fins and the shape of the fish's mouths. The dorsal fin of the Roach begins at a position directly above the pelvic fins, whereas on the Rudd the dorsal starts well behind those fins. The Roach has a slightly longer top jaw; the Rudd's underjaw is longer.

Roach are a shoal fish, often found in size/age groups that seem to remain as a unit until the breeding season, when they mix with other groups and fish of other species. The Roach spawns in the spring when the water temperature rises above 14°C. Males

Typical diet of the Roach

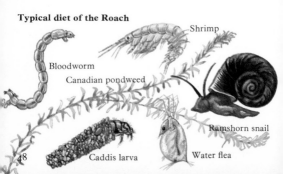

Shrimp

Bloodworm

Canadian pondweed

Ramshorn snail

Caddis larva

Water flea

Roach

become brighter in colour and mature males develop small white breeding tubercles on the head and sides. The fish tend to deposit their sticky eggs in shallow backwaters with reeded margins and little flow on the water. There the eggs adhere to weed fronds. Roach eggs hatch in about a week, and the minute larvae remain hanging on the weeds for two or three days after which the fry cluster in huge clouds trying to escape predation by small Pike and Perch.

Roach grow quite quickly, providing there is enough available food. In some waters, particularly when ill-advised stocking has taken place, the Roach remain stunted although perfectly capable of breeding after a four year maturing period!

They are a delightful fish, found in all types of water environment but best suited to a clean, fast-flowing stream where they develop hard, lean bodies with superb coloration.

Rudd

DACE *Leuciscus leuciscus*

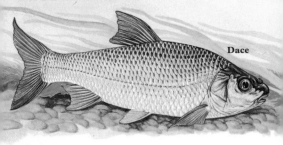

Dace

The dashing habits of this tiny fish of the streams, flashing through the sparkling water of the shallows, has given it the name 'dart'. The species is widely distributed in England, but not often seen far north of the Scottish Border counties. It appears only locally in Ireland.

Looking somewhat like a Roach, though slimmer and less colourful, the Dace does not attain the same mature size nor does it often choose to live in still waters. Dace are greenish-black on the back, with silvery sides shading to a creamy white belly. The single fins are a muted grey, while paired fins are pale yellow with an occasional reddish bloom. Both anal and dorsal fins have a pronounced concave appearance, a useful reference point when comparing the fish with immature Chub.

Dace spawn in early spring during the hours of darkness in shallow, running water. As dawn rises the breeding males drift downstream to deeper water to rest before continuing the exertion of spawning. Gravid females stay close to the chosen gravel patches until they have shed all their eggs. The eggs hatch in 2–3 weeks, depending on the water temperature. Dace are a fast-maturing species. Some are able to breed after only one year of life, though the average fish begins breeding in its second year.

Dace gather themselves into large shoals when feeding. Their diet consists of plankton when young, insects, larvae, small crustacea and algae.

Typical habitat of Dace —
a fast, shallow stream

CHUB *Leusiscus cephalus*

Chub rising to a fly

The Chub is a powerful, thickset fish, found in clean rivers and streams that offer a constant water flow over gravel or sandy bottoms. There are a few instances of still water populations, particularly in East Anglia, where they have been introduced from adjacent streams. Widely distributed in England, the species does not appear north of the Scottish Border counties or in Ireland.

The Chub is a solid, round fish with a broad head, which has led to the species being termed 'Loggerhead', an unfair title because the head is certainly not out of proportion to the body! It has a large mouth, devoid of teeth. Like all the *Cyprinidae* (Carp family of fish) the species has only throat teeth, *pharyngeals*, used to grind vegetable matter, small crustaceans and larvae. This is one member of the Carp family that will predate on small fish fry, particularly just after spawning, though fish are high on the Chub's diet most of the year.

Chub have large silver scales, with a marked dark banded edge, and a clearly defined lateral line. The upper body is deep purple-black, with silver flanks fading to a creamy belly. Both dorsal and anal fins have a convex edge (*see* Dace, p. 50); the paired, pelvic fins and anal fin exhibit a pale reddish tinge.

Chub breed in May. Like the Roach, the males grow white breeding tubercles on the head and body. The eggs are sticky and are broadcast among waterweeds and gravels. As with most of the *Cyprinidae*, Chub will hybridize with other fish that choose similar spawning territory.

ORFE or IDE *Leusiscus idus*

This beautiful small Carp was introduced from eastern Europe and Asia, as a fish for garden ponds and aquariums. The golden variety is most popular, but escapees into a natural habitat tend to revert back to the normal, Rudd-like coloration. There are some breeding populations in rivers, ponds and small lakes.

Orfe

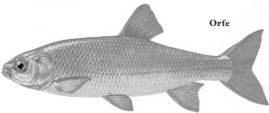

GOLDFISH *Carassius auratus*

The original ornamental Goldfish were brought to us from China in the early seventeenth century. Later introductions came from Portugal, where breeding stocks had become established after arriving from Asia. The higher water temperatures, in that country, have ensured the success of the Goldfish as a wild species. The same cannot be said in Britain, although Goldfish kept in shallow garden ponds (*see* left) will probably find sufficient heat to encourage them to spawn. Many colours and body shapes are known, but the wild fish looks something like a Crucian Carp, though less deep-bodied.

MINNOW *Phoxinus phoxinus*

Minnows are tiny silver-brown fish with vertical brown markings, sometimes confluent, along the flanks. They inhabit many fast-flowing rivers and streams throughout England, Wales, Ireland, southern Scotland and most of Europe where they are seen, in the warmer months of each year, as huge shoals, sporting just under the water's surface. The species prefers running water but will live in ponds that have clean water conditions.

Breeding begins in late May, when the males take on a brilliant red-coloured belly, and their heads become much darker. The eggs are shed among loose gravel. Only minute, planktonic food is eaten by the fry. Adult Minnows feed on water insect larvae and algae. The Minnow is an important indicator of water quality to the scientist.

GUDGEON *Gobio gobio*

The Gudgeon is found in slow-flowing rivers, with clean, gravelly bottoms, throughout most of England and Ireland. The body is a dull green-brown on the back, fading to a yellow belly, with fins that are small and delicate, though the tail fin is large, muscular and forked. A number of spots run along the upper body and lateral line.

Gudgeon spawn in May, shedding their sticky eggs among stones and waterweeds. The Gudgeon is a fish that feeds on the riverbed where young fry feed on plankton, the adults moving to a diet of larger insect larvae and crustacea, such as *Gammarus spp.*, the freshwater shrimps.

Minnow

Close-up of
Gudgeon
showing barbels

Minnow trap

Gudgeon

57

Rudd

RUDD *Scardinius erythrophthalmus*

The Rudd is certainly one of nature's most beautiful fish. Its trademark is flashing golden scales of a brilliant red hue, along the flanks and fins. Widely distributed throughout Europe, the Rudd prefers still water habitats in England, Ireland, Wales and the south of Scotland. The species can be found in running waters, but only those where the flow is gentle, and in places that offer backwaters as an escape from the full force of spates.

Rudd are summer fish. During the warm months of the year, they are easily detected in any water as they rise freely to take insects from the surface. Any confusion between the Rudd and its near relative the Roach, is soon cleared up by a close examination of the fish's mouth and dorsal fin position. In the Rudd, the bottom jaw is slightly longer than the top one. Its dorsal fin begins at a point well behind the fish's pelvic fins (*see* Roach, p. 46). Adult fish are much deeper than Roach of the same size.

Rudd, like most other *Cyprinidae*, are shoal fish. They tend to gather in groups of the same age and body size. They begin spawning in late May, or earlier if the sunshine is warm enough to heat the shallow margins. Male fish adopt brighter coloration and grow a rash of breeding tubercles on their heads and bodies. The shoals can be seen splashing and rolling among weeds where the eggs are deposited. This vigorous activity may well stimulate other species to investigate and even join in the breeding activity. Rudd hybridize with a considerable number of other species, especially when there is competition for suitable weeded spawning ground.

Female Rudd are prolific; many thousands of eggs are produced, and these hatch in just over a week. The larvae attach themselves to vegetation for a short period and then begin a life of feeding on minute organisms. Adult Rudd have an omnivorous diet, taking water insects and their larvae, small crustaceans and some vegetable matter. There is evidence to suggest that they will also eat the smallest fry of other species.

Roach × **Rudd**
hybrid

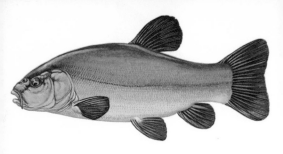

TENCH *Tinca tinca*

The Tench, like the Rudd, has a reputation for being a summer fish. But it is not a species that one will see regularly for it is demersal in habit and rarely rises to the upper water layers. Tench are widely distributed throughout southern Europe and the British Isles, with the exception of most of Scandinavia, and Scotland above the Forth–Clyde valley.

It is a fish of lakes, ponds and slow-running rivers, having a strong preference for fertile waters with a lush growth of bottom weed. This species fares well in the deep clay pits of East Anglia, and in vast waters, such as the Norfolk Broads, Holland's Friesland lakes and the Irish loughs (most of which are worked-out peat bogs of yesteryear). All these water situations offer muddy lakebeds with exceptional invertebrate populations. Like Carp, Tench can tolerate low oxygen levels, and evidence suggests that they can also exist in a water that is slightly saline. The fish can live for long periods out of water, which

Pelvic fins of male
extend past the vent

has enabled man to transport and stock the species
into many and widespread waters.

The Tench is easily recognized as it is not similar
to other *Cyprinidae*. It has a dark olive-green back,
shading gently to rich golden flanks and an orange-
yellow belly. There are countless tiny scales embedded in the skin which is liberally coated with
slime; the scales are so small that the fish may
appear scaleless. The reddish eyes are small, almost
piggish in appearance, and the fish has two barbules,
one at each corner of its mouth. Tench fins are unmistakable; large, powerful and well-rounded. This
species is one of the few freshwater fish that exhibits
a visible difference between the sexes. Male Tench
have a thickened leading edge to their pelvic fins,
which are also larger than those of the female.

Tench disappear soon after the first of winter's
early frosts. They go into a form of hibernation,
burying themselves in the bottom mud. Occasional
forays will be made in the spring on warm and sunny

Lobworm

days, but it is not until May that this species begins to take a serious interest in group or shoal activity.

Tench spawn during June and July, depending on water temperature. A large number of sticky eggs are extruded among soft waterweeds in shallow margins. The eggs hatch quickly and the fry gather in large shoals to feed on algae and minute plankton. Adult fish eat most water invertebrates, though they have a particular liking for freshwater mussels and pond snails. Growth is very slow and the species is renowned for longevity.

There are many myths concerning the healing properties of Tench slime. Isaak Walton, in his book *The Compleat Angler*, suggests that Tench act as a physician fish to Pike – a most unlikely friendship! The fish's healing powers were also extended to man, and their use is mentioned in Greek and Roman writings.

There is also a golden variety of the Tench. Probably introduced from Germany, in the middle of the last century, it has long been kept as an ornamental species. The fish's golden-scaled body is blotched with irregular brown patches.

Breadflake

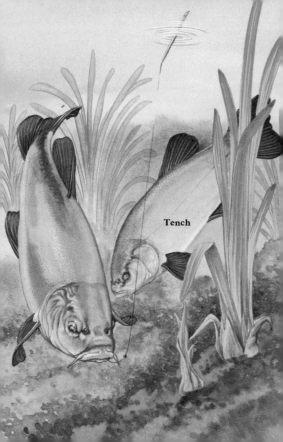

Tench

BARBEL *Barbus barbus*

Elongated, with a rounded, muscular body, this species is found in rivers that have a strong flow of water where, with its flattened belly, it is ideally suited to hugging the riverbed. The Barbel is confined to only a few river systems in England, but is widely distributed on the Continent, where it is found as far east as the Danube. There are three closely related species living in Spain, Northern Italy and the Balkans.

The Barbel is a member of the *Cyprinidae* and possesses four pronounced barbules, two on the extremities of the upper jaw and one in each corner of the mouth. Its fins are large and powerful, with a trace of reddish hue at the junctions with the body. The dorsal fin has a serrated edge to the stiffened, leading ray. Barbel are bronze-green in colour, with clean, defined scales and a noticeable lateral line.

They spawn in early summer, among stones and loose gravel, after a migratory journey to upstream shallows. Male fish have white breeding tubercles in evidence. The species feeds on tiny invertebrates, insect larvae and snails, foraging during the dark hours among the detritus swept along by the current.

BLEAK *Alburnus alburnus*

This small, silvery-scaled fish forms huge shoals, swimming just under the surface in clean, slow-flowing rivers and streams. There are still water populations, but only as a result of introduction by fishermen. Found in Europe and England, the Bleak forms the staple diet of many freshwater predators.

Its claim to fame is that the scales were once used in the production of artificial pearls. In the 1650s a Frenchman, Jaquin, discovered that the scales of this tiny, Sprat-like fish, formed a sediment which he used to coat glass beads.

BITTERLING *Rhodeus sericeus amarus*

A small European fish, although there have been localized introductions into England. This colourful, bronze-green species has a brilliant metallic stripe along the hind flanks, which is exaggerated in the male fish, at spawning time. The female has a long ovipositor with which she deposits a few eggs in each open freshwater mussel that she comes upon. The

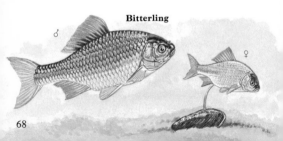

Bitterling

male fish ejects milt into the surrounding water; this is drawn into the mussel as it respirates.

SILVER BREAM *Blicca bjoerkna*

Found throughout Europe, the Silver Bream is confined to local still waters and slow-moving rivers in East Anglia. It is a delicate, small fish that never attains the colouring or size of the native Common Bream. The eyes are large and the single fins are a muted grey colour, with occasional pinkish tinges to the junction with the fish's body. This species has an extremely slimy feel to it and the scales are easily rubbed off. It spawns in June among weeds in muddy shallows and, in Europe, is known to hybridize with other Bream species.

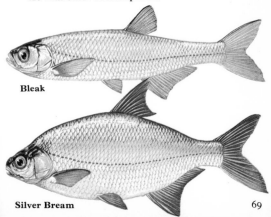

Bleak

Silver Bream

COMMON or BRONZE BREAM
Abramis brama

A gregarious fish found throughout Europe and the British Isles, though rarely north of the Scottish Border. It is known as a still water species but has a tolerance for slow-flowing currents found in lowland, meandering rivers. Bronze Bream form huge shoals that graze the underwater vegetation like sheep, ever moving in their quest for sufficient food. The presence of a shoal is easily detected by the immense clouds of bubbles and coloured water sent to the surface as the fish feed.

When young, Bronze Bream look rather like the silver species (*see* p. 68). They both have a silvery, insipid, appearance but, when weighing about a pound (0.45 kg), the Common Bream takes on a darkened, deep-brown back with bronzed flanks and a creamy belly. Mature fish have a pronounced hump, beginning behind the head, curving up to the dorsal fin. The tail fin is markedly forked and the anal fin is long with a concave edge.

Bream spawn in May, choosing shallows with lush weed growth. They prefer the hours of darkness for this activity, which is noisy and involves a tremendous splashing and rolling of their bodies. The eggs are sticky, adhering to the plant growth where they hatch in about 14 days. The larvae remain attached to plants for a period before starting to feed on plankton. Juvenile growth is fast in warm waters, and the adult fish can attain huge weights.

Common Bream

CARP *Cyprinus carpio*

This species, the largest of the Carp family (*Cyprinidae*), was introduced to Britain and western Europe as a food source for humans. The implantation came as early as the thirteenth century, because Dame Juliana Berners, in her book *A Treatyse of Fysshynge wyth an Angle** mentions the species. The Carp is native to the Far East where it has been successfully domesticated for centuries.

Only the juvenile fish form shoals; adults, especially the huge specimens, adopt solitary behaviour. This species favours well-weeded, still-running rivers, lakes and ponds with deep water. There is a considerable tolerance to low oxygen levels, so many of the smallest farm ponds and irrigation ditches will make a perfect home for this creature. Growth can be fast, particularly when accelerated by warm water such as is found in many rivers where power stations pump back cooling water!

Carp have been subjected to selective breeding by man, which has resulted in colour/scale aberrations.

* Dame Juliana Berners's book, believed published in 1486, was thought to have been written considerably earlier.

Leather Carp

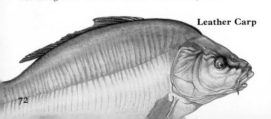

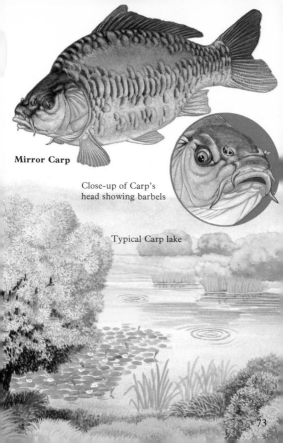

Mirror Carp

Close-up of Carp's head showing barbels

Typical Carp lake

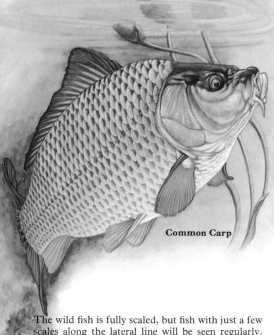

Common Carp

The wild fish is fully scaled, but fish with just a few scales along the lateral line will be seen regularly. These are called **Mirror Carp**. Yet another variety, **Leather Carp,** have no scales on them at all. There are four barbules present in all varieties, two sprouting from the fish's upper lip and one at each corner of the rubbery mouth. The fins are large and powerful. Colour varies with the variety; the Common

Crucian Carp

Carp (the fully-scaled fish, p. 74) has a purple back, shading to golden sides and cream underparts; Mirror and Leather Carp are less colourful.

The species spawns in June among weeds in shallow areas. Many eggs are shed and these hatch in a week or so. The larvae proceed to feed immediately on plankton. They grow quickly, measuring over 4 inches (10 cm) long at the end of their juvenile year. The carp attains sexual maturity in 3–5 years and can live 20 years or more.

CRUCIAN CARP *Carassius carassius*

This small, deep-bodied fish can be readily identified by its lack of barbules and huge, sail-like, convex dorsal fin. Like the Common Carp, the species is an introduction into Britain, probably from Germany, and prefers still waters and slow-flowing rivers. It breeds in summer and will hybridize with the larger Common Carp.

STONE LOACH *Noemacheilus burbatulus*

Stone Loach

Loach are tiny nocturnal fish that live amongst stones, weedgrowth and debris at the bottom of small rivers and streams with a constant flow. Stone Loach show intolerance to the smallest amount of pollution, and are distributed throughout England and Ireland. They are blotchy brown in colour, often with a yellowy marbling, and rarely exceed 4 inches (10 cm) in length. The dorsal and tail fin have dark spots in a patchwork pattern. Stone Loach have six barbules; four as a fringe to the upper lip and one at each corner of the mouth.

SPINED LOACH *Cobitis taenia*

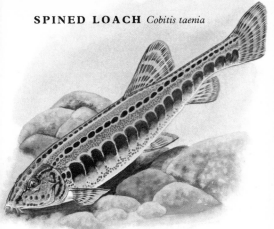

Spined Loach

The Spined Loach will be found in still waters and muddy, slow-running rivers where it feeds on minute organisms among the detritus. The species is confined to eastern Britain, although widely distributed in Europe. This little Loach has a fringe of four smaller barbules hanging from the upper jaw, with a further two barbules, one in each corner of the mouth. Paler in ground colouring than the Stone Loach, the blotching is less pronounced and there is a row of dark spots, beginning behind the gill case and extending to the tail. This scavenger fish is kept by aquarists.

Wels

WELS or CATFISH *Silurus glanis*

An introduction from Europe, the Wels (*see left*) is a
night-feeding fish that inhabits muddy lakes and
slow-flowing rivers. It can grow to a length of at
least 5 ft (1.5 m). Black or dark bronze-grey in colour,
the unmistakable identification feature is the fish's
barbules: six on the head, two of which reach back
beyond the pectoral fins. Catfish are carnivorous,
eating fish, amphibians and small swimming mammals.

BURBOT *Lota lota*

A rarely seen member of the Cod family (*Gadidae*),
the Burbot (below) is confined to freshwater in
eastern England, though some authorities consider
it extinct. The species is common on the Continent;
it is found during the night, feeding in still waters
and rivers.

Burbot

Freshwater Eel

FRESHWATER EEL *Anguilla anguilla*

Few fish have a more fascinating life story than the Eel. This begins in the western Atlantic, where the adult fish that have travelled from Europe meet to spawn. After hatching, the larvae, or leptocephali, that look something like a transparent leaf, begin a migration to the north-east carried on warm ocean currents of the North Atlantic Drift.

On the journey, the leptocephali metamorphose into transparent, Eel-shaped creatures. Drifting

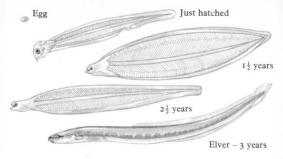

Egg   Just hatched

1½ years

2½ years

Elver – 3 years

Metamorphosis from egg to elver

along with the currents means a long journey to
northern waters; 3–4 years is the average time before
the Eels arrive off European river mouths. There
they undertake another bodily change, becoming
elvers, with a muted, silver-grey appearance. They
ascend into rivers where they are caught in millions.

As they grow, by feeding on larvae, crustaceans
and the fry of other species, Eels adopt a yellow
colouring on the sides and belly. Nobody can state
an accurate age for when Eels become sexually
mature, but there is evidence to suggest that the
length of the Eel is a good indicator. Female fish
begin moving downriver when they attain a length
of 2 ft (0.6 m), whereas male fish start their seaward
journey when only just over 15 inches (0.4 m) long.*

Some members of the species will not enter freshwater at all, preferring to stay within the confines of

estuaries and saltwater inlets. As the Eels prepare for the migration back to their spawning grounds, they become black on the back with silver flanks. The eyes enlarge and the jaws take on a pointed shape, possibly due to the Eel's lack of need to continue feeding while on the breeding journey.

Both elvers and adult Eels are said to migrate across land, between watercourses and enclosed still waters that have no connecting streams. It is distinctly possible, after periods of heavy rainfall, that there is sufficient moisture for the Eels to wriggle across fields, and even roads.

* Alwynne Wheeler, *The Fishes of the British Isles and North-West Europe*, suggests that male Eels spend 7–12 years feeding and growing in freshwater. Female Eels are credited with a longer maturing span of 9–19 years.

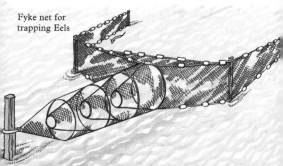

Fyke net for trapping Eels

Yearly migration route from Sargasso Sea

Key – Green: drift line from Sargasso Sea
Red: path of mature Eels back to
Sargasso Sea

STICKLEBACKS

Sticklebacks are pugnacious little fish. The males build nests and jealously guard both eggs and surrounding territory.

These are a group of extremely small fishes; the Three-spined Stickleback is tolerant of saline conditions, the Ten-spined prefers to spend its entire life in freshwater and the Fifteen-spined lives permanently in saltwater. Sticklebacks are widely distributed in European waters and around the British Isles.

Three-spined Stickleback *Gasterosteus aculeatus* is a favourite fish among small boys who search the ponds and streams with their nets and jam-jars. It is a colourful fish that can also be found in estuaries

15-spined Stickleback

and along the shoreline. At the spawning season, male fish adopt a bright red throat and belly and build a nest into which they attract a succession of mature females to lay their eggs. The male fish then guards the eggs and tends the newly-hatched fry.

The **Ten-spined Stickleback** *Pungitius pungitius* loves the stagnant farm pond or weed-choked stream but can, on occasion, be found in brackish waters. It grows to a slightly smaller size than the Three-spined Stickleback. The remaining species, a **Fifteen-spined Stickleback** *Spinachia spinachia*, is wholly marine (*see* p. 190).

3-spined Stickleback

PERCH *Perca fluviatilis*

A widely distributed species, found in most European countries with the exception of northern Scotland and Norway. The Perch is a predator and, like the Pike, regulates the number of fish contained in a water. Perch tend to feed on small fry and do not appear to scavenge.

The Perch is a boldly coloured fish having a purple-black back, green-grey flanks and a white belly. Older fish have a deep, compressed body with a pronounced hump in front of the dorsal fins. Fins on the fish's underside have a reddish tinge. The easily recognizable features of this species are the vertical, dark bars on the sides and the two dorsal fins; the first has about 15 sharp spines with a black blotch on the rear end; the second, much smaller dorsal fin, has 15 or so soft, branched rays.

Perch spawn in May when the large breeding female fish are attended by a few smaller males. The eggs, many thousands in number, are extruded as filamentous strands, woven among weed and sunken branches in shallow water. These pearl-like eggs, draped over underwater vegetation and glistening in sunlight, are easily seen by waterfowl who consume large quantities of each year's spawn. Even so, the Perch is a survivor; waters can soon become crowded with shoals of stunted Perch which, though finding hardly enough food to grow, are still capable of reproduction.

Perch

ZANDER or PIKE-PERCH
Stizostedion lucioperca

This is a species from eastern Europe. There are other closely related fish in North America and Europe, where the various species are highly regarded for the quality of their flesh. Zander are not widely distributed in British rivers and drainage canals. The Zander has gained a reputation for killing vast quantities of shoal fish in the Fenland district of England, where the species was deliberately introduced to a number of rivers that drain this agricultural area. Conditions in these drainage waters suit the life style of the Zander as it is tolerant of muddy water. The species has taken over the role of the Pike as a population regulator in turbid waters. They will rarely be found in the company of Pike, a species that chooses clear-water situations when it can.

The Zander is a sleek, silvery-green fish with small scales. It has large fins and a forked tail. The dorsal fins are clearly divided; the first is supported by spines and the second is composed of soft rays with just two spines in the leading edge. The anal fin also has a couple of spines before the soft rays. A number of spots can be distinguished on the upper fins and tail. A Zander's teeth are sharp and those at the front of the mouth are long and slightly recurved.

Zander breed in the spring, from May onwards when the temperature is above 16°C. They spawn amongst waterweed and on gravelly shallows. This species is totally predatory in behaviour; as fry, they eat larvae and tiny crustaceans, and as they grow their diet changes to fish.

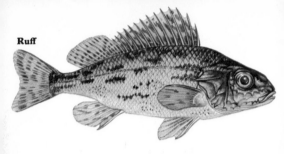

Ruff

RUFFE or POPE *Gymnocephalus cernua*

A small fish that looks much like a juvenile Perch, the Ruffe can be found throughout Europe and eastern England. It is a shoal fish of still waters and slow-running rivers where it will be found in the deeper areas that are shaded from direct sunlight.

Ruffe are green-black on their backs, shading through grey-green to an off-white belly. The fins are large and the dorsal fins, the forepart of which is spined, are joined. The fish's eyes are large and purple in colour, a good distinguishing feature that separates the species from young Perch. Ruffe feed on the smaller invertebrates, young amphibians and insect larvae.

LARGE-MOUTH BLACK BASS
Micropterus salmoides

There are two similar species of this North American genus forming part of the Sunfish family; the Large-mouth and the Small-mouth Black Bass. The former

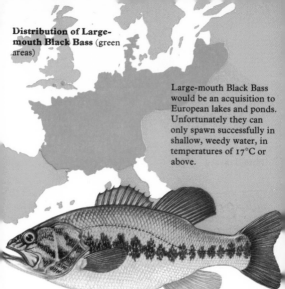

Large-mouth Black Bass would be an acquisition to European lakes and ponds. Unfortunately they can only spawn successfully in shallow, weedy water, in temperatures of 17°C or above.

Large-mouth Black Bass

has been successfully introduced in Europe, where it has spread through many waters as a result of its sportfishing potential. Minor introductions have been made into a few discrete English lakes. The fish is bronze-green, with a few dark bars on the sides and gill case. The spined and soft-rayed dorsal fins are joined with a pronounced dip between them.

91

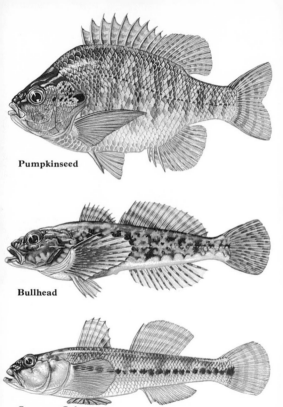

Pumpkinseed

Bullhead

Common Goby

92

PUMPKINSEED *Lepomis gibbosus*

Another introduction from North America into Europe, where this small colourful fish is found in weeded still waters and slow-running streams; it has a tolerance for shallow, warm conditions. The Pumpkinseed has been put into a few English waters, probably by amateur aquarists who found themselves with an excess of juveniles, as the species is a prolific breeder.

BULLHEAD or MILLER'S THUMB
Cottus gobio

A tiny nocturnal species found in Europe, Scandinavia and England, it is a shy brown-marbled fish that lives among stones and thick waterweeds. The head and forepart of the body have a flattened appearance. The fins are large with a division between the two dorsals. Bullheads have a spine on the top of the gill cases. During the spring spawning, the male parent guards the eggs which are laid in a nest scraped out from among the fine gravels.

COMMON GOBY *Pomatoschistus microps*

A small shoalfish found in fresh, slow-flowing waters and around the coast in the littoral zone. It is the only member of the Goby group of fish that will enter freshwater. Its dorsal fins, the first of which is spined, are separated and the fish's pelvic fins are fused together to form a weak sucking pad, with which it can adhere to stones. The male fish guards the eggs after spawning, which may happen several times in a season.

The marine environment

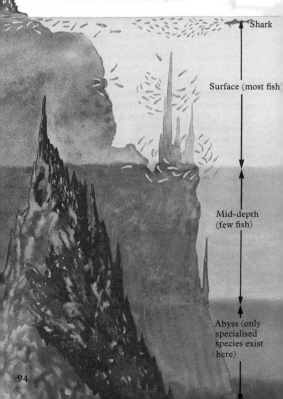

Shark

Surface (most fish)

Mid-depth (few fish)

Abyss (only specialised species exist here)

94

Looking out from the shoreline, we can divide the sea into three zones: the splash zone is nearest to the land mass, the littoral zone then extends out to the edge of the continental shelf and, lastly, the true ocean. Each zone has a depth significance as a fish habitat. The splash zone is only just covered, at the highest of spring tides, by enough water to wet or splash the vegetation and animal life – but rock pools will be formed and replenished. In the littoral zone we find most of our fish living in depths of up to 1200 ft (366 m), the depth at which the continental shelf ends. Here the continental slope begins, inclining down rapidly into the abyss where the depth is measured in miles and strange deepwater fish abound!

Some fish are described as pelagic, or surface-dwelling. Demersal species are those that choose to live and feed on or close to the seabed. Between these two extremes there are countless habitats and the necessary fishlife to fill them.

An example of fish finding their own level is an offshore reef, that rises out of deep water to within a few feet of the surface. Feeding over the tip of the reef will be pelagic fish. Midwater species will be living down in the rock crevices. Swimming at the reef base will be the true demersal species. One cannot say with accuracy where a particular species ought to be found, other than to suggest that certain families of fish will occupy well defined locations of depth and light. There must always be some overlap, especially when we consider juvenile fish, that have yet to occupy an adult niche in the ecosystem.

Porbeagle Shark

Mako Shark

Porbeagle tooth

Mako tooth

PORBEAGLE SHARK *Lamna nasus*

A cold-water fish found throughout the Northern Hemisphere at most times of the year. The species is fond of establishing its own territory, especially over offshore reefs. Mainly found off the western shores of the British Isles, the Porbeagle Shark may follow Herring and Mackerel shoals. When resident in a rocky environment, the diet is Pollack.

The Porbeagle is a portly shark, with dark blue-black upper parts, shading to a dirty white belly. Almost cylindrical in shape, the fish has a smooth-flowing roundness to its body. The fins are large and powerful, giving this Shark incredible speed through the water. There are two horizontal 'keels' at the junction of the tapering body and tail fin. The upper lobe of the tail is largest and there is a notch near the tip. The fish's eyes are noticeably large, which suggests that the Shark has the eyesight for hunting over murky, weeded ground rather than feeding in the pelagic layers of the open ocean. Porbeagle teeth are sharp and wedge-shaped. There is a small 'cusp', a minor ridge, on either side of each tooth.

MAKO SHARK *Isurus oxyrinchus*

An oceanic, pelagic fish that migrates to North Atlantic waters in high summer. The Mako is a larger-growing species than the Porbeagle with a far wider distribution. Sleek in shape, with a deep blue upper body shading quickly to pure white under-parts, this Shark has only one horizontal keel and lacks basal cusps on its sharply pointed teeth. Both Porbeagle and Mako Sharks bear live young.

Mackerel

Plankton

BASKING SHARK *Cetorhinus maximus*

A huge, harmless fish of the upper water layers, it is
often seen by holiday-makers as it slowly patrols the
coastal current line in high summer. The Basking
Shark is a plankton feeder, and on this minute food
can attain a weight of over three tons (3048 kg).
Fish 30 ft (9.14 m) long are not unusual. Basking
Sharks are usually seen in family groups and often
vary in coloration. The adult fish are a dark brown
with lighter flanks; juveniles have a softer, muted
back with fawn flanks and belly. There can be light
blotches of colour on fish of all ages. The Basking
Shark cannot really be confused with any other fish.
It has five enormous gill slits, that appear to circum-
navigate the body. They begin on the top of the
fish's back extending to just under the throat.

Little is known about the Basking Shark's breeding behaviour. The gestation period is thought to be
in excess of two years, when only one or two infants
are produced. There appears to be a modicum of
parental care; a pup in constant contact with a particular adult has often been witnessed.

THRESHER SHARK *Alopias vulpinus*

The easiest Shark to recognize because of its gigantic, scythe-like tail fin. The Thresher Shark visits the North Atlantic area during the summer, travelling as far north as the Norwegian coast, although it would seem that we only see the smaller specimens of this species. In tropical waters, the Thresher Shark can be as heavy as one ton (1016 kg)! Threshers are not frequent inshore visitors, though there seem to be localized habitats. It is a pelagic Shark, often seen on the surface harrying shoals of Pilchards and Mackerel where it 'rounds up' the baitfish by thrashing its tail and rapidly circling them. The species is ovoviviparous, producing one or two live young each breeding season.

HAMMERHEAD SHARK
Sphyrna zygaena

The Hammerhead Shark is another unmistakable fish. It is a frequent visitor from more southerly, warmer climes where it has a number of closely-related species. The head is small with the eyes placed on the outer extremity of a flattened oblong. The nostrils are on the corners of the head, just in front of the eyes. Hammerhead Sharks have a smaller mouth than our other Shark species of the same relative size. It has a sleek, streamlined body and can grow to over 16 ft (4.9 m) long. The fish is ovoviviparous and is said to produce about 30 pups at each breeding season.

Thresher Shark

Hammerhead Shark

Close-up of eye of Hammerhead Shark

Blue Shark

BLUE SHARK *Prionace glauca*

The most common of our summer Shark visitors, it arrives off the coast of Cornwall in late June. During exceptionally warm summers the species will migrate as far north as Norway. Blue Sharks are slim fish, up to 16 ft (4.9 m) long, with large pectoral fins. They are pelagic feeders, following shoals of Mackerel, Pilchards and Sardines on the warm currents that press northward from the tropical region. When seen in the water, or immediately after being boated, the species is a deep, rich blue on the back that lightens to an azure on the flanks, fading to a snow-white belly. They are beautiful fish but their colour soon disappears when left to dry in the sun.

The fish is viviparous, having a primitive placenta joining the eggs to the uterine wall. A large litter of pups is expelled, their size and number depending on the length and maturity of the mother.

SMOOTHOUNDS

We find two closely-related species of Smoothound in North Atlantic waters. The **Smoothound** *Mustelus mustelus* is a thickset Dogfish with large fins and a total absence of any spots on the body. The **Starry Smoothound** *Mustelus asterias* is similar in shape but has a heavy sprinkling of white spots across the back and along its flanks. Both are slow-moving, demersal species with crushing jaws ideally suited for a diet of crustaceans.

Mustelus mustelus is viviparous (the developing young have a rudimentary placental connection from the egg yolk sac to the oviduct wall), whereas *M. asterias* is ovoviviparous. The young develop from the egg, within the oviduct, without any connection.

SPURDOG *Squalus acanthias*

The most common of the small Sharks to inhabit our waters, Spurdogs travel in huge, predatory shoals and feed on smaller species. This Shark makes a large contribution to the wet fish trade. Thousands of tons are fished each year and the boneless flesh is sold as 'Rock Eel'. It is a streamlined fish, pale grey in colour with a few lighter spots along the sides. There is no anal fin present. Each of the dorsal fins has a sharp spine at its leading edge.* Spurdogs are ovoviviparous, producing up to a dozen pups each breeding season.

---

* Some scientists suggest that the spines have a venomous gland in the furrow at the back of the spines. Others claim that the tissue, which partially shields the spines, could be toxic. Either way, a wound made by mishandling a Spurdog can be very painful and often requires medical treatment.

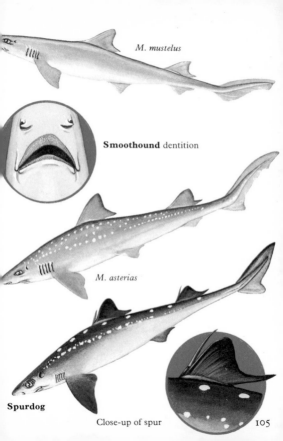

M. mustelus

Smoothhound dentition

M. asterias

Spurdog

Close-up of spur

105

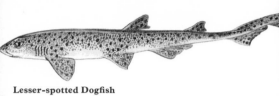

Lesser-spotted Dogfish

Bull Huss

Mouth of
Greater-spotted
Dogfish →

Mouth of
Lesser-spotted
Dogfish

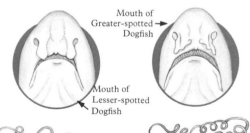

Egg case of
Dogfish

106

BULL HUSS *Scyliorhinus stellaris*

This small Shark is often described as the Greater-spotted Dogfish or Nursehound. It is a fish of southern British waters and the European coast, and is demersal in habit, quartering rock-strewn sea-bed habitats for a mixed diet of crustaceans and small fish. It has a striking appearance: almost black on its back, the fish's flanks are fawn, blotched with an uneven dark brown pattern. The Bull Huss lays eggs, contained in a capsule the colour of brown seaweed. At each corner of the rectangular case is a spiralled tendril which is used to attach the egg cases on to kelp and weeds. Young Bull Huss are several inches long when they emerge from the capsules after a growing period of many months. Searching of the low spring tideline will often produce a Dogfish 'purse'.

LESSER-SPOTTED DOGFISH
Scyliorhinus caniculus

This is a much smaller Dogfish, often given the name Roughhound, because of its abrasive skin texture. It is more widespread in distribution and numbers than the Bull Huss.

This nocturnal, bottom-dwelling little scavenger will literally eat anything. Unlike its larger relative, it tends to avoid rough ground preferring to scour the open sands, muddy estuaries and weeded shallows. The fish is less colourful, having a mass of dark brown blotches over its brown body. It is also egg-laying, although the capsules are much smaller in size. When picked up the fish has a nasty habit of wrapping itself around an arm, which can tear skin off!

♀

TOPE *Galeorhinus galeus*

The Tope is a small, fast-swimming brown-grey Shark that haunts the inshore, shallow waters of the British Isles and European seaboard. It is fairly widespread in distribution and there are related species around the world. Locally, it has become a source of food for humans. The fish is slender, with smallish fins and a distinctive deeply-notched tail. The Tope's head has a flattened shape, when viewed from above, and its eyes are quite large. There is a nictitating membrane present, moving from the front to the rear of the eye.

Tope are demersal fish. They feed on the smaller shoal species and flatfish which they find in inshore areas. The species is known to hunt in a pack when Mackerel are plentiful. Tope frequent sandy bays and inlets as found on the South Wales coast, Cardigan Bay, Thames Estuary, the Wash, More-

combe Bay, Solway Firth and a number of well-known sea areas in Ireland. The fish's teeth are sharp and have a serrated edge at the back. Tope are viviparous, breeding in summer when they produce about 30 pups, though small females would expel considerably less offspring. It is interesting to note that the large fish that swim into inshore waters are usually gravid females moving in to where it is thought they have their young. There is a total absence of male fish accompanying the females at this time. It is possible that the females view the males as predators on the pups.

A female fish of 75 lb (34 kg) was landed at Tenby, South Wales some years ago; male Tope rarely exceed 30 lb (13.6 kg) in weight. The fish's skin, when cured, is extremely tough and has been used as a form of leather; it is also used as a smoothing material for cabinetmakers and other woodworkers.

Thornback Rays

♂

♀

Egg case
of Ray

THORNBACK RAY *Raja clavata*

The first of our Skates and Rays, the Thornback Ray is a widespread species that favours inshore waters of shallow depth. It can be found on storm beaches in a few feet of water, although the 30–60 ft (9–18 m) line is a more certain depth.

The Thornback Ray has a pronounced wave to the leading edge of its wings. It is more angular than other Rays.* Two small dorsal fins are placed far back on the fish's tail. The species shows a wide variation in colouring, though a drab grey-brown is usual, and a number of darker blotches or spots may be present. The spines are placed as a single row running along the spine and tail, flanked by secondary rows at either side of the tail. There may be a patch of spines towards the extremity of each wing and, sometimes, a smaller patch on the underside of the wings. Rays have crushing teeth, ideal for feeding on crustaceans, but will eat almost anything.

All Skate and Rays are fertilized internally and the resulting eggs are expelled in leathery, brown capsules called 'mermaid's purses'.

* The body of all Skates and Rays is compressed, giving them a flattened shape. This distinctive appearance has given rise to confusion as to what a flatfish is! Basically, flatfish – such as Plaice and Flounder – are compressed sideways and they swim on their sides. The dark body colour and eyes are on one side of the fish. Skates and Rays are compressed from spine to belly through their bodies and swim with their bellies to the seabed. Body coloration is on the upper side as are the eyes and spiracles.

BLONDE RAY *Raja brachyura*

A locally common Ray of southern and western sea areas, the species is usually found in depths of about 120 ft (37 m), but immature specimens will feed almost up to the tideline. A Blonde Ray's body is covered with small dark brown spots on a light brown ground. These spots extend to the extreme margins of the wings. On adult fish the upper, coloured body is often seen to be liberally dotted with fine spines. Few thorns are present and are confined to the tail.

Blonde Ray ♀

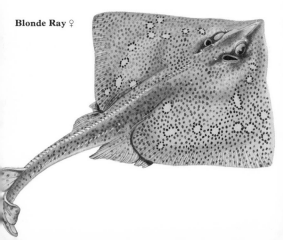

SPOTTED RAY *Raja montagui*

Although closely resembling the former species, the Spotted or Homelyn Ray has larger speckles of dark colour and these do not extend out to the wing margins. Some adult fish will display a light, circular patch surrounded by dark spots on the wings, known as an ocellus. The species does not attain the size of either the Thornback or Blonde Ray, and rarely exceeds 7 lb (3.2 kg) in weight. There are spines along the spinal ridge and on the inner leading edge of the wings. This fish has only a few irregular thorns on its body.

Spotted Ray ♀

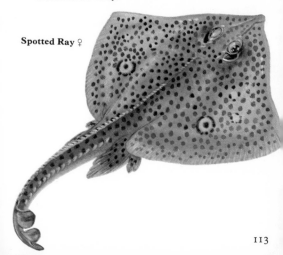

Starry Ray ♂

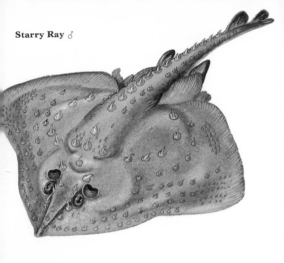

STARRY RAY *Raja radiata*

This species has a more northerly distribution and favours slightly deeper water. It is a prolific fish that forms a major part of trawled catches. Creamy-brown in body colour with a smattering of light patches and black spots, the Starry Ray has a rough upper surface covered in sharp spines. There is a clearly defined line of large curved thorns running from behind the fish's eyes back to the dorsal fins. Like most Rays it feeds on crustaceans but live fish are also taken.

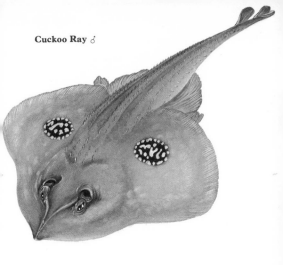

Cuckoo Ray ♂

CUCKOO RAY *Raja naevus*

This is a readily identifiable Ray. The two circular
yellow and black ocelli, lying on a body ground
colour of pale brown, are distinctive. The fish has no
large thorns, only patches of small spines on the
upper surface and two rows of thicker spines along
each side of the tail. It attains a weight of only about
5 lb (2.27 kg) but is fairly common. Cuckoo Rays are
found in depths of 60 ft (18.3 m) and over. They are
distributed around the British Isles, down to the
Mediterranean.

SANDY RAY *Raja circularis*

This larger-growing species has a northern and western distribution, where it is found in deep, off-shore waters. Rich brown in colour, the fish has a number of perfectly symmetrical light spots on the wings. The fish's upper surface has patches of fine spines and there are two rows of stout, curved spines either side of the tail. There are no median line thorns present. Little is known of the life style of this oceanic species, although many Sandy Rays are brought ashore as part of commercial boat catches.

SMALL-EYED RAY *Raja microocellata*

The Small-eyed or Painted Ray, as it is often called, is southerly in distribution. The species is rarely found north of south-west England, and Ireland. Its common name refers to the fact that the fish's eyes are much smaller than in other species. The title 'Painted Ray' is applicable as this fish displays a mass of light, wavy marblings on a pale cream or yellowy background. The spines are grouped closely along the tail, towards the snout of the fish.

UNDULATE RAY *Raja undulata*

This fish is found on similar sandy seabed habitats to the former species. It also displays waving patterns of colour but these are opposite in form being dark chocolate brown, with white spotted edgings, on a mid-brown body. Both species attain a relatively small adult size.

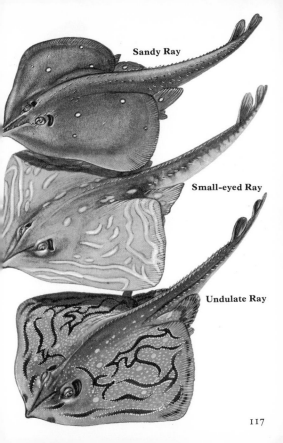

Sandy Ray

Small-eyed Ray

Undulate Ray

TORPEDO RAY
Torpedo nobiliana

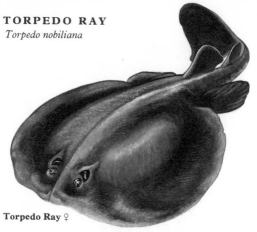

Torpedo Ray ♀

The Torpedo Ray is an uncommon summer visitor to southern and western inshore waters of the British Isles and French coast. The body is round, dark or muddy blue, with large pelvic, dorsal and tail fins. The Torpedo Ray has no sharp thorns or spines. It has the reputation of delivering a high voltage electric shock if handled. It may be that the fish uses this weapon to stun its live fish prey or as a security against attack by larger predators!

There is no biological difference between Skates and Rays. The anatomical differences can be simply defined as Skates having long noses and a distinctive diamond shape – whereas Rays have short noses and a more circular body shape. Skate grow much larger than any of the Rays.

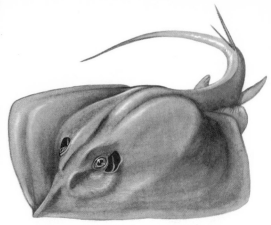

Sting Ray ♂

STING RAY *Dasyatis pastinaca*

Another dangerous member of the Ray family, Sting
Rays are often found on the east coast of Britain in
the warmer months, lying in shallow water or around
offshore sandbanks. This species possesses a single,
serrated stinging spine growing from the upper
surface of the whip-like tail. Occasionally specimens
are seen that have more than one of these spines
growing from a common root position. The wound
caused by the sting is painful and can cause severe
discomfort or death.

Close-up of mouth

Common Skate

COMMON SKATE *Raja batis*

The Common or Grey Skate is widely distributed in the north Atlantic Ocean from Iceland south to Portugal. It lives in deep water of 100–900 ft (30–270 m). A fairly common fish, this Skate achieves a large body size and weight but is only second in size to the White Skate.

Common Skates have a dirty grey or brown appearance on the upper surface. Some adult fish will have a marbling of lighter and darker patches of colour. The belly is never white but has a pale grey background, liberally dotted with darker blotches and spots. Immature specimens have no spines or noticeable thorns. Male adult fish, distinguished by their claspers, have spines over the upper disc area; female fish only have spines around the head and leading edge of the wings. Both sexes have spines under the snout. Adult Skates have at least one row, possibly more, of hard thorns along the spinal ridge and tail back to the dorsal fins.

Skates are demersal fish, feeding on crustaceans and small fish on or close to the seabed. They trap their prey by flopping their huge wings down over the creature while they manoeuvre the prey towards their mouth. Skates are fertilized internally and the female ejects a number of leathery capsules containing the egg.

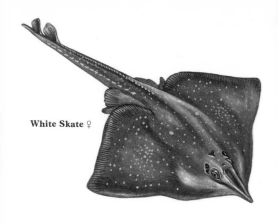

White Skate ♀

WHITE SKATE *Raja alba*

This species frequents more southerly waters than
the Common Skate. It is found regularly off the
Atlantic coast of Ireland and is the largest growing
of the three indigenous species, said by commercial
fishermen to grow to at least 8 ft (2.4 m), giving a
possible body weight of over 500 lb (227 kg). White
Skates have a more pointed snout, often described as
bottle-nosed, and the leading edge of the wings has
a convex bulge. The underside is pure white, which
serves as its prime identification point.

Long-nosed Skate ♂

LONG-NOSED SKATE *Raja oxyrhynchus*

The smallest and least common of our three Skates,
the long-nosed species can be readily separated by
its exceptionally elongated snout and deeply concave
leading edge to the wings. Its life style is similar to
the Common Skate and it is found in the same
environments, although adult fish appear to have a
liking for deeper water. The dorsal colour is dark
brown-grey, with light and dark brown marbling;
the belly varies from dirty grey to almost black with
patches of black spots or streak marks.

SPRAT *Sprattus sprattus*

The Sprat is a pelagic species widely spread over the eastern Atlantic. It closely resembles the Herring but is much smaller and deeper in the body when adult. Identification features are the saw-edged belly and the position of the pelvic fins, which originate in front of the leading edge of the dorsal fin.

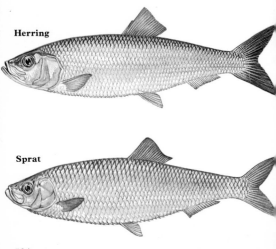

Herring

Sprat

Herring drifter

HERRING *Clupea harengus*

This fish is one of the most important food species to humans. Under enormous commercial fishing pressures, the Herring manages to survive in huge shoals across the whole of the North Atlantic. There are several associated species in other parts of the world. Herring are pelagic fish, feeding on plankton and minute fish fry. They show a remarkable tolerance towards waters of low salinity; frequently Herring shoals can be seen in estuaries where they attract large numbers of marine and avian predators. They engage in long migrations annually to seek food and to spawn.

PILCHARD *Sardina pilchardus*

Although looking very like a Herring, this fish has two distinct identification features; radiating streaks on each gill case, and a rounded belly. Pilchards exhibit a southerly distribution, ranging from the Mediterranean up to the English Channel. It seems that they replace the Herring as a food fish in temperate and sub-tropical waters. They are pelagic in habit and feed exclusively on plankton. The Pilchard is a valuable food fish, both fresh and canned. When immature, they are called Sardines.

Anchovy

ANCHOVY *Engraulis encrasicolus*

A small, silvery fish of southerly distribution, travelling seasonally to the North Sea. At one time it was known to shoal in vast numbers in the Ijsselmeer (Zuyder Zee) before barrages were erected to prevent the ingress of saltwater. The mouth is a different shape to all the other Herring-type fishes.

Ring-netting for Pilchards

Pilchard

GARFISH *Belone belone*

The Garfish is a streamlined, slender fish, built for speed. Oceanic in distribution, the species visits inshore waters in high summer. Often Garfish are seen in the company of Mackerel shoals as both species are pelagic feeders, harrying shoals of fry that swim just under the surface. Like the Mackerel, Garfish are extremely fast swimmers, renowned for leaping clear of the water. Easily recognized by its elongated beak, which is full of sharp teeth, the Garfish has a green upper body which shades to a creamy belly. The scales are tiny and the lateral line is positioned

Garfish

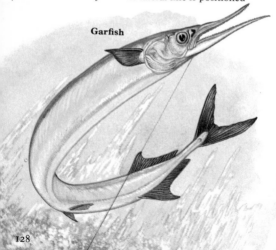

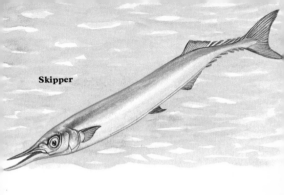

Skipper

rather low on the fish's body. Garfish have green bones, which causes them to be viewed with suspicion as a table fish, although they are succulent.

SKIPPER *Scomberesox saurus*

A pelagic-feeding summer visitor from warmer waters, the Skipper or Saury Pike does resemble a Garfish until one looks closely at the beak and fins. The Skipper's beak is much shorter, relative to the length of the fish's body. Its underjaw is slightly longer than the upper part of the beak. Both jaws contain a series of very small teeth. The fish's anal and dorsal fins have an anterior section made up of finned rays, with the remaining parts formed as small finlets. The fish's common name is derived from its habit of skipping, lightly, out of the water to clear obstacles or escape from predators.

129

CONGER EEL *Conger conger*

The Conger Eel is a fish that people love to hate. This may be caused by its snake-like appearance or because of the fixed, almost hypnotizing stare that the Eel gives people; it is definitely a species that deserves to be handled carefully. The mouth is full of very sharp teeth and a Conger Eel can live out of water for an extended period, biting long after it appears dead! This Eel, which can grow to over 100 lb (45 kg) in weight, varies in colour depending on the habitat in which it lives. Over open ground, with just a smattering of weeded rocks, Congers have a grey back and almost white belly. Living in wrecks and on reefs, the Conger Eel may be nearly totally black. The dorsal fin extends from behind the fish's head to the tip of the tail. The anal fin is much shorter and begins close behind the vent.

The Conger Eel has a similar life history to the Freshwater Eel in that it undertakes a once in a lifetime journey, over vast distances, to the breeding ground. There, in the deep waters near to Madeira, it spawns in mid-water and dies. After hatching, the larvae drift on warm ocean currents north-east to the European shores. The journey takes 2–3 years, and during the latter part of the passage the tiny creatures undergo a metamorphic change, which is completed as they arrive in littoral waters. Immature Conger Eels appear to favour shallow inshore environments where, no doubt, they feed on small crustaceans found there.

As adults the diet changes to larger prey, lobsters, edible crabs and live fish. This nocturnal-feeding Eel lives in dark holes and among rocks and weeds, ideal ambush points for what is a demersal and fairly slow-moving species. Harbour walls provide cracks and crevices for the Conger to occupy, particularly if there are working fishing boats using the port. The attraction is waste fish falling into the water. Larger Eels live offshore in deep water, where wrecks and reefs are a favoured habitat, providing a 'larder' of live fodder fish.

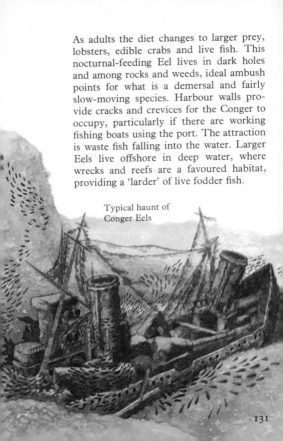

Typical haunt of
Conger Eels

Conger Eel

Underside of male Pipefish showing pouch with eggs

PIPEFISH

There are six species of Pipefish found in the littoral waters of the European coasts. The genus *Syngnathus* has three species; *S. typhle* the **Broad-nosed Pipefish**, *S. acus* the **Great Pipefish** and *S. rostellatus*, **Nilsson's Pipefish**. There are two species within the genus *Neophis*: *N. lumbriciformis* the **Worm Pipefish** and *N. ophidion* the **Straight-nosed Pipefish**. One other species remains, *Entelurus aequoreus* the **Snake Pipefish**, which is oceanic in habit and relatively uncommon in shallow water.

Pipefish are all similar in appearance; their most significant characteristic is that the male incubates the eggs. He gathers the eggs after the female has expelled them; they are then either contained in a pouch under the belly, or adhere to the abdomen of the male parent. Male Pipefish within the genus *Syngnathus* keep both the fertilized eggs and the hatching young in their pouches until the fry attain a length of about 0.8 inches (2 cm). Pipefish can be found standing upright among eelgrass and other seaweeds where they feed on minute shrimps, fish fry and planktonic animals.

Great Pipefish in eelgrass

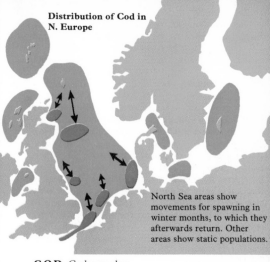

Distribution of Cod in N. Europe

North Sea areas show movements for spawning in winter months, to which they afterwards return. Other areas show static populations.

COD *Gadus morhua*

The Cod ranks first among the world's food fish. It is widely distributed in arctic and temperate waters on both sides of the Atlantic Ocean where the species lives over the continental shelf and in the shallow coastal waters. Cod are shoal fish, making long migrations in search of food and at spawning time. They grow to enormous sizes; one landed in America weighed over 200 lb (90.7 kg). The average size for European fish seems to be 10–40 lb (4.5–18.1 kg).

Typical coloration of Cod

137

Cod are demersal in habit but will frequently leave the seabed to predate among Herring and Sprat shoals. In winter, when Sprats are shoaled up near to the coastline, large groups of Cod will swim in very shallow water following their prey.

The fish shows widely varying coloration which is mainly conditioned by environment; a remarkable yellow marbled pelage speckled with brown streaks when migratory, and a red or dark brown colouring when the non-migrating fish is immature and living among inshore rocks and weedbeds. Both colour forms have a defined broad white lateral line which takes on a gentle curve over the pectoral fins. Cod have three dorsal fins and two anal fins. The head of the Cod is large; in adult specimens it appears to be almost one third the body length. In old and spawning fish the belly sags, giving the underparts a drop-sied appearance. There is an elongated barbule below the Cod's chin and the upper jaw extends well beyond the lower. The fish's lips are thick and rubbery.

The Cod is a scavenger. Its diet will include almost anything edible and a lot of things that are not. There are many records of bottles and stones being found in the stomach of this species. The fish probably swallowed these items because there was a sea anemone or shellfish attached to them, which was the important food item that it wanted. Crustaceans form a large part of the food, as well as molluscs and echinoderms. Inshore the Cod feeds over marine worm beds; fish, when available, may be added to its diet.

Female Cod are prolific spawners. The eggs expelled are measured in millions. Cod eggs are pelagic; hatching time varies with ambient temperature but 12 days is the average for British waters. After a few months spent feeding on plankton in the upper layers the larvae swim to the bottom to begin their demersal life.

'Red' reef Cod A red, non-migratory coloration can be seen amongst Cod that live over inshore weeded reefs.

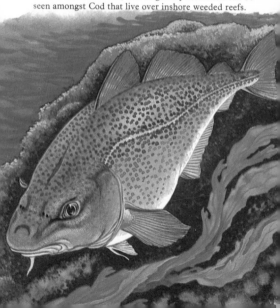

Haddock

HADDOCK *Melanogrammus aeglefinus*

At one time the Haddock was almost as important to commercial fisheries as the Cod. The species is distributed widely in the North Atlantic from the Arctic Circle down to the north Portuguese coast, but man's appetite for this fish has ensured the demise of former huge shoals. The Haddock is not a large-growing fish, rarely exceeding 10 lb (4.5 kg) in weight. It is demersal in habit and forms up into travelling shoals that favour feeding over soft sea-beds where there are colonies of shellfish and crustaceans, such as scallops, mussels, prawns and small crabs.

The Haddock has a blue-brown back with silvery

flanks and a black, curved lateral line. The fish has an elongated upper jaw with a barbule below the chin. It has a black blotch just above the pectoral fins. The fish's first dorsal is sharply pointed and the tail deeply forked. Haddock spawn from winter to late spring after migrating into deep water. Following the protracted breeding period, they return to shallow inshore waters.

Trawling for Haddock

POUTING *Trisopterus luscus*

A widely distributed small Cod that tends to favour the warmer sea areas of Britain and the Bay of Biscay, the Pouting has little commercial value. Small in size, the fish is deep-bodied, with a bronze ground colour, dark brown back and vertical bars of darker shading. The pelvic fins and first dorsal are long and sharply pointed. The tail is square-cut. It is noticeable that the Pouting has large eyes and a long barbule, which gives this fish the common name of Bib. The species inhabits rough ground, reefs and wrecks and feeds on shrimps, small crabs and tiny fish.

Pouting

WHITING *Merlangius merlangus*

Widely distributed over the North Atlantic from the Arctic Circle down to the Mediterranean, this species swims in huge, predatory shoals over soft seabeds where it feeds on small fish and crustaceans. The Whiting is a slender, silvery member of the Cod family that lacks a barbule. It has a mass of spiky teeth, used to grasp live prey. The anal fin is longer than in the Pouting, and the pelvic fins are elongated, possibly acting as organs of touch. Whiting mature in their third year and spawn in the spring. Although not the most popular food fish, the Whiting is an important food species.

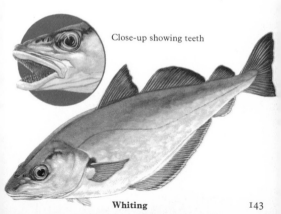

Close-up showing teeth

Whiting

Coalfish

Pollack

POLLACK *Pollachius pollachius*

Pollack are fish of the rough seabed, preferring to haunt offshore reefs and areas of broken ground, striking from ambush points among thick kelp. They are found around the British Isles, but chiefly in western areas of clear water. The fish has splendid coloration; a red-brown back that shades to golden flanks. There is a distinctive dark lateral line, that looks rather like a strand of twisted thread, curving over the pectoral fins. The Pollack's lower jaw is considerably longer than the upper one and there is no barbule present. Pollack predate on small fish but will feed on plankton in the evening, when the fish exhibits a vertical migration. The species spawns in the early spring.

COALFISH *Pollachius virens*

Similar to the Pollack, this species has a more northerly distribution and favours deeper water. Immature fish, known as *billet*, remain inshore and are locally common. The Coalfish is more rounded in shape with jaws that are almost equal in length. It has a rudimentary barbule that is hardly discernible in adult fish. The body ground colour appears to be rich black, with a definite greenish sheen. The Coalfish's white, straight lateral line identifies it best from the Pollack. Coalfish are found right across the Atlantic Ocean, whereas the Pollack is a European species. It is almost entirely predatory on other fish, notably the Herring.

POOR COD *Trisopterus minutus*

A small member of the Cod family with a distinct resemblance to the Pouting, the Poor Cod has a reddish colouring and lacks both the vertical bars of darker shading and any form of dark blotch at the root of the pectoral fins. Poor Cod rarely exceed 10 inches (0.25 m) in length. They are found almost everywhere in the North Atlantic. Although favouring rocky bottoms, the species will range over sand and muddy seabeds in its search for microscopic food and minor invertebrates.

TORSK *Brosme brosme*

A fish of northern waters, the Torsk frequents deep waters off the Scottish coast. This fish has only one dorsal fin which, along with the anal fin, is fused with the fish's tail. Torsk have an elongated barbule beneath the chin. Demersal in habit, this species mainly feeds on crustaceans. The fish spawn in very deep water, where a huge number of eggs are shed.

BLUE WHITING *Micromesistius poutassou*

A fish of the open ocean, the Blue Whiting inhabits deep water where it feeds on crustaceans and tiny fish. Looking something like the common Whiting, this species is slimmer and the three dorsal fins are spaced further apart. The underjaw is noticeably longer and the fish's eyes are large. The Blue Whiting is a future source of human food but, as yet, little harvesting of the fish takes place. At present, fish are used to process into fishmeal.

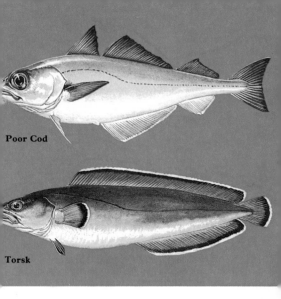

Poor Cod

Torsk

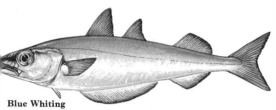

Blue Whiting

Ling

LING *Molva molva*

The Ling is found throughout the eastern Atlantic
on a rough seabed and in deep water. Probably the
largest-growing of the Cod group, it inhabits reefs,
wrecks and areas that provide excellent ambush
opportunities. The species lives an almost solitary
existence. Ling, when mature, do not form shoals.
The fish is dark brown-black on the upper parts,
with silvery flanks. Mature fish have a mottling of
dark blotches on their sides. This species has one
anal and two dorsal fins, with a clear white banding
around the frilled, outer edges. Ling have a large
barbule under the chin and the mouth is full of sharp
teeth, indicating that they are predators on other fish.
Ling are prolific spawners, laying up to 60 million
eggs in late spring. They form a large part of the
Northern Hemisphere's production of smoked and
dried fish.

Hake

Close-up of mouth

HAKE *Merluccius merluccius*

This species is found in the North Atlantic as far south as Portugal. It has been subjected to massive overfishing with the result that few Hake are caught today. They are a mid-water species that is almost entirely fish-eating. The Hake is another of the Cod family with only two dorsal fins and an elongated anal fin. It is less Eel-like than the Ling and has no barbule. The mouth is large and possesses extremely sharp teeth. Hake scales are large and distinct and are easily removed by abrasion.

149

GREATER FORKBEARD
Phycis blennoides

A species that is thinly distributed in the open Atlantic but very common in the Mediterranean. It lives in deep water and forms large shoals. The fish has two dorsal and one anal fin. Its pelvic fins are reduced to thin, trailing appendages that flow rearwards to touch the anal fin. A dull brown on the upper body shades to a white belly. The Greater Forkbeard has large eyes and a long barbule on its chin.

Greater Forkbeard

TADPOLE FISH or
LESSER FORKBEARD *Raniceps raninus*

This rare minor Cod inhabits shallow waters where it lives a solitary existence among rocks and kelp. In appearance it looks something like a tadpole as the body is dark brown in colour with a large and flattened head. The first dorsal fin is composed of only a few short rays. The second dorsal fin and the anal fin are both extremely long. The fish has a small barbule and thin, elongated pelvic fins.

Tadpole Fish

151

THE ROCKLINGS

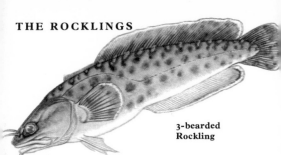

3-bearded Rockling

The Rocklings are a group of secretive fishes related to the Cod family. The behaviour and chosen environments vary enormously between the different species. Bodily, there are very few anatomical differences. The Rocklings resemble immature Ling and are often mistaken for the young of that larger, deepwater fish. There are five Rockling species distributed around the British Isles and North Eastern Atlantic:

Three-bearded Rockling *Gaidropsarus vulgarus*
Four-bearded Rockling *Rhinonemus cimbrius*
Five-bearded Rockling *Ciliata mustela*
Northern Rockling *Ciliata septentrionalis*
Shore Rockling *Gaidropsarus mediterraneus*

Northern Rockling

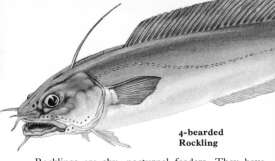

4-bearded Rockling

Rocklings are shy, nocturnal feeders. They have large mouths with sharp teeth. Each species has two dorsal and one anal fin. The first dorsal fin is rudimentary and lies folded in a cleft on the fish's back. The number and position of barbules on the upper jaw varies between species; only the single chin barbule is common to all.

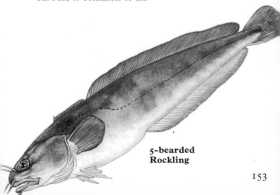

5-bearded Rockling

Sunfish

SUNFISH *Mola mola*

This is a peculiar fish with one dorsal and anal fin, and no evidence of a tail. It is deep-bodied and flattened laterally with the rear part of the body ending in a muscular frilling. Though a weak swimmer, it has a worldwide distribution. The Sunfish is carried along on the ocean currents, making sluggish paddling movements with its fins. The fish has a tiny mouth and feeds pelagically on slow-moving larvae in the plankton layers.

OPAH *Lampris guttatus*

Often called the Ocean Moonfish, the Opah is distributed worldwide. A beautifully coloured fish, with a purple-blue ground and vermillion-red fins, it is deep and laterally compressed. The mouth is small with thick, rubbery lips capable of tubelike extension. Opah are pelagic fish that drift northward during the summer months on the warm current stream. The main diet is said to be squid found among the plankton. They are rarely seen but are caught, accidentally, in surface nets.

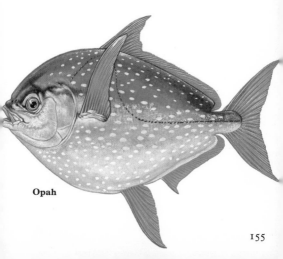

Opah

JOHN DORY *Zeus faber*

A striking fish of unique shape and colouring, the John Dory has a deep body which is laterally compressed. The mouth is huge and shoots forward into a kind of suction tube. There are two dorsal fins, the first of which is supported by stiff spines. There is a single spine in the pelvic fins and four in the first section of the anal fin. The dark blotch on the flanks makes identification certain. This species favours warm, shallow waters.

BOARFISH *Capros aper*

Similar in shape, the Boarfish has larger eyes and a 'pig snout'; hence its name! The fins are spined but the fish lacks the vivid colouring of the John Dory.

Boarfish

John Dory

HORSE MACKEREL or SCAD
Trachurus trachurus

This widely-spread visitor is no relation to the true
Mackerel but can often be found accompanying
Mackerel shoals inshore. It is a member of the family
Carangidae, a large family of sporting fishes found in
tropical waters. The Scad can be identified by the
row of bony plates found along its flanks. The fish
is greenish-grey in colour, with a spined first dorsal
fin and two sharp spines ahead of the anal fin. The
tail is deeply forked and the pectoral fins curved,
ending in a sharp point. There is a dark blotch high
on the gill case. The species spawns in the summer
and fry are frequently found sheltering among the
tentacles of the jellyfish *Rhizostoma*. It is thought
that the fry feed on jellyfish parasites and in turn are
offered protection from predators by the jellyfish's
stinging tentacles!

Scad

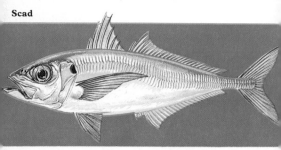

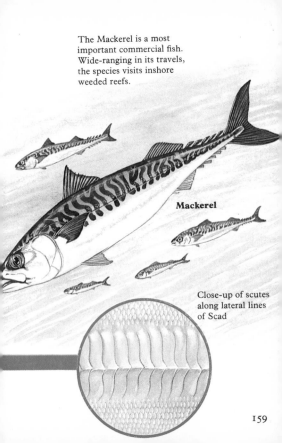

The Mackerel is a most important commercial fish. Wide-ranging in its travels, the species visits inshore weeded reefs.

Mackerel

Close-up of scutes along lateral lines of Scad

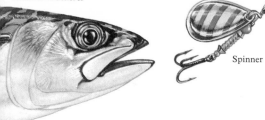

Spinner

MACKEREL *Scomber scombrus*

One of the fastest swimmers in the sea, the Mackerel
is a member of the Tunny family. The species can be
regarded as pelagic-feeding, ocean wanderers for
much of each year. In early summer huge shoals
move into the shallow, coastal waters to harry the
fry of other species. Then, as autumn and winter
arrive, the fish leave for deeper water offshore.*

Mackerel are unmistakable in shape and colouring. Built for speed, they are streamlined with small
fins some of which fold into grooves on the body, so
presenting less surface drag as the fish speeds through
the water. The tail is deeply forked and there are tiny
finlets on the back and belly after the second dorsal

* Here the Mackerel find no security, for massive predation
by deep-water trawling in winter by a number of European
countries has decimated the once-prolific shoals. The
Mackerel is one of our best known table fish and the demand
for ever-increasing catches is formidable.

Gulls feeding on brit driven to surface by Mackerel

and anal fin. There is also a sharp spine behind the fish's vent which, though hard to detect, can easily cut into a person's hand. A pair of keels can be seen at the root of the tail. Mackerel do not possess swim bladders. The Mackerel's streamlining is particularly noticeable around the fish's head; the mouth can be tightly closed against the ingress of water and the eyes are set in sockets, flush to the head, so as not to protrude outside the tapering body shape.

The colour of a Mackerel, fresh from the sea, is hard to describe. On the back, the fish has a brilliant metallic greeny-blue sheen. This ground colour is patterned, dorsally, by a mass of black twisting lines. On the lighter, pale green flanks there are blotches of deeper colour and the white underparts have a number of scales that catch the light, flashing with a myriad of hues.

RED MULLET *Mullus surmuletus*

The Red Mullet is a species with a misleading common name; the fish belongs among the tropical Goatfish family, and is found in shallow waters of the Mediterranean and European coast, north to southern England and Ireland. Identification features are its colour, flattened forehead and long trailing barbules, which are used to detect its food (small invertebrates and other life found in mud and sand).

Red Mullet

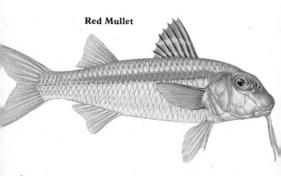

RAY'S BREAM *Brama brama*

This fish is known worldwide but can only be termed

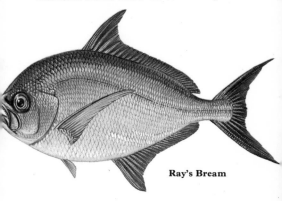

Ray's Bream

a sporadic visitor to the British Isles. It is very common off the coasts of Spain and Portugal. Single specimens are washed ashore, mostly in winter, perhaps due to exceptional warmth in north-flowing currents earlier in the year. This was noted by the naturalist, John Ray, who gave the fish its common name in the seventeenth century. The fish is deep in the body and laterally compressed, indicating a life spent at considerable depths. A deep brown in colour, the flanks have a metallic, flashing quality to the scaling. Note the vicious teeth.

163

Bass

Lugworm

Ragworm

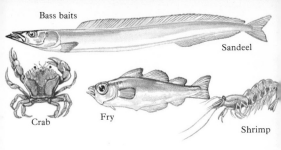

Bass baits

Sandeel

Crab

Fry

Shrimp

BASS *Dincentrachus labrax*

This is one of the best known sporting fish. Renowned for feeding in the breaking surf of the open storm beaches, the Sea Bass is found on most European southern and west-facing shores. It is a warm water species in the British Isles, tending to be found in shoals on western Atlantic shores as far north as the Solway Firth. It is widespread on the south coast and moves up into the North Sea to the Yorkshire coast and Friesian Islands of Holland. The more northerly areas attract solitary but large specimens, whereas warmer sea areas are populated by smaller, 'school' Bass.

The Bass has a tolerance for brackish water and will often be found in the estuaries of large rivers. Here it can be seen searching the mudflats for invertebrates and crustaceans. This behaviour tends to produce a confusion with the Grey Mullet, who look similar and frequently swim in shallow water with their dorsal fins cutting the surface.

Bass are powerful fish, with thickset, muscular

bodies. They are dark green-black on the back with silvery flanks and a creamy belly. The scales are hard and rough to the touch, with a spiny, ctenoid hind margin. The first dorsal is spined, the second has soft, jointed rays. There are also three spines at the leading edge of the fish's anal fin and a single spine on each of the paired, pelvic fins. The edge of the gill case has a sharp plate, which can slice an unwary finger inserted to lift a fish by the gills.

Little is known about the fish's spawning time or behaviour.* Ripe fish are taken in the winter on Irish beaches and empty mature females are found on the shores of southern England at the same time. It may be that Bass spawn over a protracted period, shedding a number of eggs when and where conditions appear favourable. Still less is known about the annual migration to deep water; some winter catches have been made off the Eddystone Rock, suggesting that this predator seeks the food availability of large offshore reefs during the cold months. On the Atlantic shores of Ireland, Bass are present throughout the winter, the warmer oceanic water offering a more stable environment. They are slow to mature and over-fishing is endangering the species. Efforts to curb the commercial fishing pressures have yet to produce any worthwhile results.

---

* Dr Michael Kennedy, in his book *The Sea Angler's Fishes* is inclined to disagree with the view that Bass spawn offshore in deep water but is in favour of the speculation that Bass spawn inshore by instalments, thereby never presenting us with an opportunity to obtain a concentration of eggs and newly-hatched larvae.

Storm beach – haunt of Bass

Distribution map and summer migration from the Mediterranean Sea of Sea Bream

BLACK SEA BREAM
Spondyliosoma cantharus

A summer visitor to North Atlantic waters, but widely distributed in the Mediterranean. It has been most often recorded from the English Channel, off the Sussex and Hampshire coasts. The body is deep and compressed, purple-grey in colour with streaks or horizontal bands of golden scales below the lateral line. There is no dark spot above the pectoral fins (*see* Red Sea Bream). The dorsal fin is long with 11 spined rays and 12–14 soft, branched rays.

RED SEA BREAM *Pagellus bogaraveo*

This fish has a similar distribution to the Black Sea Bream, though it can be found in more northerly areas. Identification points are the red fins, golden-red scales, large eyes and a dark shoulder patch. It travels in shoals and frequents rocky ground.

Red Bream

Black Bream

Typical wrasse habitat

BALLAN WRASSE *Labrus bergylta*

This species is found in shallow water around the rocky coastline of the European Atlantic. Coloration varies tremendously with green, brown and red predominating. Under the throat there is often an orange patch, and some fish exhibit a lattice-work

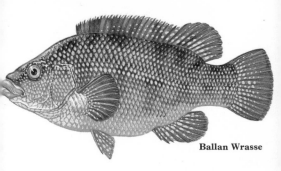

Ballan Wrasse

pattern of red-brown lines across the shoulders and head. The Ballan Wrasse is a solid, thickset fish with large fins and clearly defined dark-edged scales. The dorsal fin has spined rays in the forepart with a lesser number of soft branched rays in the posterior section.

The Ballan Wrasse feeds on molluscs and crustaceans found among the boulders and kelpbeds of the littoral zone. Its lips are extremely prominent and the teeth are chisel-shaped, used to tear limpets and other molluscs from rock faces. It breeds in early summer, building untidy nests made of tufted seaweeds bound together with mucus, in rock crevices. During the winter, Ballan Wrasse escape the cold, to which they are extremely sensitive, by retiring to deeper water offshore that offers a rocky ground habitat.

♂

CUCKOO WRASSE *Labrus mixtus*

This is a slimmer, more colourful member of the
Wrasse family with a longer snout. Like the Ballan
Wrasse, the gill case is scaled and the jaw teeth
strong and pointed. There are powerful, grinding
molars at the throat entrance. Cuckoo Wrasse display a sexual colour difference which in former times
caused problems of identification; male fish are
brilliant blue on the head and upper body, with a

♀

belly and fins of bright orange hue. Streaks and a marbled pattern of darker blue can be seen extending back from the fish's head and gill case. Female fish are reddish-orange with dark blotches beneath the rear section of the dorsal fin.

Less common than the Ballan Wrasse, the Cuckoo Wrasse is found in similar habitats but in much deeper water. Often this smaller Wrasse will be caught in lobster and crab pots, from which it steals the bait.

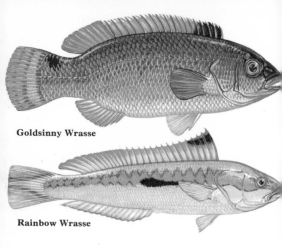

Goldsinny Wrasse

Rainbow Wrasse

GOLDSINNY *Ctenolabrus rupestris*

A very small member of the Wrasse family that lives in shallow, coastal waters. The species is widely distributed in areas with a rocky seabed. This fish can be identified by the dark blotch at the beginning of the dorsal fin and a similar spot at the top of the fore-edge of the tail fin.

RAINBOW WRASSE *Coris julis*

Alone among the Wrasse, the Rainbow Wrasse has sharply-pointed fins and lacks scaling on the gill case and cheeks. Colouring is variable; males have purple-green upper parts, shading to silvery-yellow

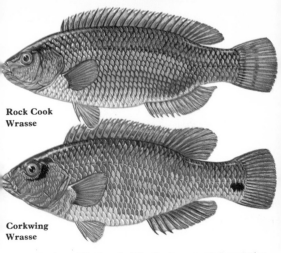

Rock Cook Wrasse

Corkwing Wrasse

flanks, while female fish display a muted variation with narrow, lighter, lateral stripes.

ROCK COOK *Centrolabrus exoletus*
A small Wrasse found in more northern climes. It has a small mouth and there are five spined rays in the fore-edge of the anal fin.

CORKWING WRASSE *Crenilabrus melops*
This small fish resembles the Ballan Wrasse, though *C. melops* is more thickset, often with two dark blotches of colour; one at the root of the tail and the other at the rear of the fish's eye.

WEEVERS

These fish are venomous. They can inflict a painful wound with their spined dorsal fins, that have poison sacs located at the base. The first dorsal spine is the dangerous one and care must be taken to avoid the spines on the gill case of the Greater Weever.*

* Medical advice should always be sought if you are stung by a Weever or similar-looking fish.

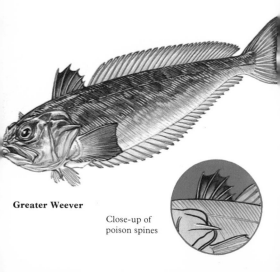

Greater Weever

Close-up of
poison spines

Found in shallow water, in places where there are gently sloping sandy beaches, the **Lesser Weever** *Trachinus vipera* is a tiny species measuring only 7–8 inches (18–20 cm) in length. It lies partly buried in the sand, with the dorsal spines erected. Weevers feed on minute invertebrates and fish larvae. The **Greater Weever** *Trachinus draco* grows to two or three times the size of its smaller relative. It is a slimmer fish with spots and streaks over a grey-blue body colour. It frequents deeper water offshore.

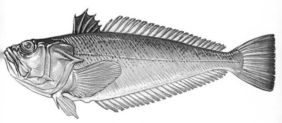

Lesser Weever

WOLF-FISH *Anarhichas lupus*

An ugly fish, the species is found on both sides of the
North Atlantic Ocean in temperate and arctic seas.
This large bottom-dwelling fish is often called a
Catfish or Sea-cat. Its chosen environment is deep
water over a rocky seabed. The fish has a long, frilled
dorsal fin extending from behind the head, back to
the tail. The anal fin begins at the vent and ends just
below the posterior edge of the dorsal. The pectoral
fins are huge rounded paddles. There are no pelvic
fins present and the fish's scales are rudimentary.
The body colour is drab green-grey, with faint
brown marbling on the flanks and fins.

A Wolf-fish's head is blunt and the large mouth is
furnished with curved canine teeth on the upper and
lower jaws. Behind the lower canines are a series of
smaller molars. There are also teeth in the roof of the
fish's mouth. This fearsome armoury is needed to
cope with the demersal crustaceans: crabs, lobsters
and shellfish, that form the bulk of this fish's diet.

Wolf-fish are highly prized among commercial
fishermen as the flesh is tasty and the fish can grow
to a considerable size: fish of 8 ft (2.4 m) and more
have been landed. They form a large part of the
catch in northern waters, taken by seine nets and on
longlines. In the fish market they are sold as 'Rock
Salmon', a title that is also shared by the ubiquitous
Coalfish.

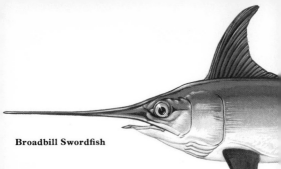

Broadbill Swordfish

BLUEFIN TUNNY *Thunnus thynnus*

A pelagic oceanic hunter that travels widely, preying on shoals of baitfish. The Tunny prefers warmer climes, though after spawning this species does migrate into northern seas to feed. It can be up to 1500 lb (680 kg) and is a food fish of worldwide importance, rarely seen inshore.

Bluefin Tunny

BROADBILL SWORDFISH
Xiphias gladius

Allied to the Tunny and Mackerel, the Swordfish has an elongated upper jaw formed into a flattened bill. There are two widely spaced dorsal fins and a small keel on either side of the tail wrist. Many tales are told of Swordfish that have attacked wooden ships, but the occurrences were probably accidental.

BLUE-MOUTH *Heliconelus dactylopterus*

This fish is more southerly in distribution and is found in deep water around the Scottish coast and off the west of Ireland. Very similar in appearance to the Norway Haddock, it can be identified by the bright blue colour inside the mouth, and the very large pectoral fins.

Bluemouth

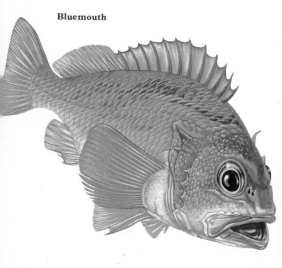

NORWAY HADDOCK *Sebastes viviparus*

A stumpy, thickset fish, brilliant red in coloration. It is an occasional visitor to Northern Scotland, where it is found in deep water over a rough seabed. It has a spiny gill case and first portion to the dorsal fin. The huge eyes dominate the large head. Norway Haddock are live-bearers of young.

Norway Haddock

Red Gurnard

RED GURNARD *Aspitrigla cuculus*

The Gurnards are fish that possess armoured bones
covering their heads. Their pectoral fins are divided
into two distinct sections. The three leading rays are
separate, stiffened tactile organs that are also used
to aid walking around on the seabed! The first dorsal
fin is tall and spined and Gurnard tails are deeply
forked. The Red Gurnard has a series of vertical
plates along the lateral line. This species is found in a
wide variety of habitats within European-Atlantic
waters.

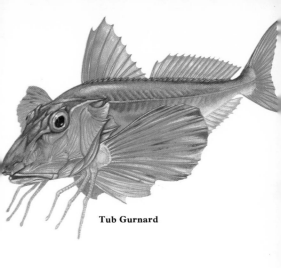

Tub Gurnard

TUB GURNARD *Trigla lucerna*

A larger-growing Gurnard but scarcer than its red
cousin. This species comes into shallow waters more
readily. The colour is variable, which causes identification problems but the huge pectoral fins, stretch-
ing rearwards beyond the fish's vent, are distinctive;
bright orange with an edging of brilliant blue. There
may also be a number of dark blotches on these fins.
The Tub Gurnard has an almost smooth lateral line,
with only a slight ridging effect.

GREY GURNARD *Eutrigla gurnardus*

The most common of the Gurnard family, found as far north as the Arctic Circle. This small fish has a prickly lateral line and a series of prickles at either side of the groove into which the dorsal fins set. Colour is variable from grey to a dull red, usually with lighter spots on the back and flanks. Found in shallow water during summer months, the fish, like all other Gurnards, is said to 'croak' when taken from the water. This noise is produced by the swim bladder and is used, presumably, to signal to other fish.

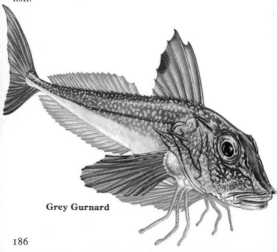

Grey Gurnard

LANTERN GURNARD *Aspitrigla obscura*

A rare deep-water species distinguished by its first dorsal fin which has a much higher second spine than any of the other Gurnards. The **Piper Gurnard** *Trigla lyra* also favours deep water. It has long spines protruding back from the gill cases above the pectoral fins, and there are connected spines that form forward projections from the upper jaw. A blunt head, streaks of colour and vertical lines on its body identify the **Streaked Gurnard** *Trigloporus lastoviza*; it is a widely distributed fish in European waters.

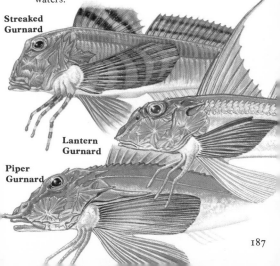

Streaked Gurnard

Lantern Gurnard

Piper Gurnard

SEA SCORPIONS

These are small, colourful fish with numerous spines on the body, gill case and first dorsal fin. The **Short-spined Sea Scorpion** or **Father Lasher** *Myoxocephalus scorpius* inhabits littoral waters, where it feeds on invertebrates and fish larvae. Both this fish and the **Long-spined Sea Scorpion** *Taurulus bubalis* lay their eggs in clumps, which the male fish guards until they hatch.

DRAGONET *Callionymus lyra*

A common, slender fish of shallow sandy areas. The male is highly colourful with an elongated, spined first dorsal fin. His mate is drab brown with smaller fins.

Dragonets

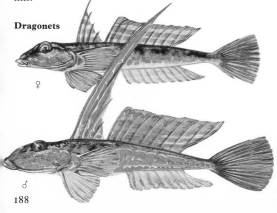

♀

♂

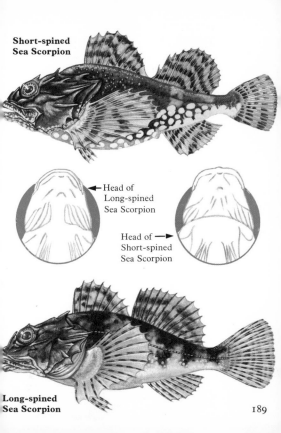

Short-spined Sea Scorpion

← Head of Long-spined Sea Scorpion

Head of → Short-spined Sea Scorpion

Long-spined Sea Scorpion

SEA STICKLEBACK or
FIFTEEN-SPINED STICKLEBACK
Spinachia spinachia

The Sticklebacks are unique in that there are two species that favour living in freshwater, one of which will also be found travelling down to feed in estuarine waters (*see* p. 84). The third, *Spinachia spinachia*, spends its entire life cycle in the North European coastal waters. This fish is very different in body shape; it has from 14–17 spines preceding the dorsal fin, which is positioned halfway along the slender body. Colour varies according to the chosen rocky habitat but olive-yellow predominates.

Sea Sticklebacks build nests among clumps of seaweed, tying the fronds together with mucus. The species, unlike the other Sticklebacks, forms a pair bond, the female depositing her eggs in the nest which the male fish guards avidly.

Nest of 3-spined Stickleback

Nest of 15-spined Stickleback

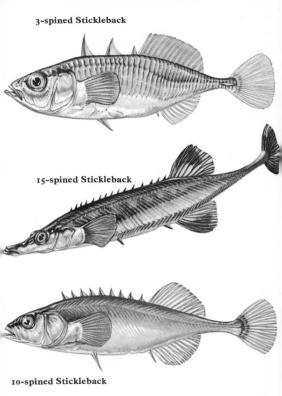

3-spined Stickleback

15-spined Stickleback

10-spined Stickleback

191

BLENNIES

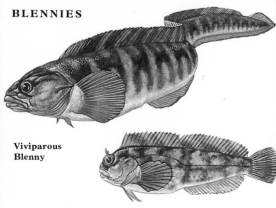

Viviparous Blenny

Tompot Blenny

VIVIPAROUS BLENNY or EELPOUT *Zoarces viviparus*

A very common fish of European littoral waters that can be found hiding among seaweeds and stones in the algal zone. The dorsal fin is continuous between head and tail, its posterior section is low and includes a number of weak spined rays. Colour varies with the fish's environment but is generally an olive-brown base with darker marbling. Fertilization of the female is internal and she produces up to 250 live young that are immediately able to swim and feed on minute invertebrates and inshore plankton.

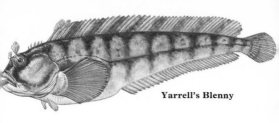

Yarrell's Blenny

Montagu's Blenny

YARRELL'S BLENNY *Chirolophis ascanii*

Another small fish of rocky, inshore waters where it lives among the seaweeds. The body is long and slender with two tentacles on the head, above the fish's eyes. There are more tentacles on the tips of the first dorsal fin spines. The colour is reddish-brown with dark mottling along the flanks.

Montagu's Blenny *Coryphoblennius galerita* and the **Tompot Blenny** *Blennius gattorugine* are two other minor species that share the common name of Blenny. Both species are small and thickset, with tentacles above their eyes.

GOBY

A large family of small coastal-dwelling fish that thrive in shallow waters. They are able to cope with powerful wave action as they have pelvic fins fused together to form a suction pad which allows the tiny fish to stick themselves to rocks or other supports. The eggs are laid on weeds or in open shells, where they are guarded by the male fish.

The **Painted Goby** *Pomatoschistus pictus* has two rows of highly coloured spots on its dorsal fins and brown blotches along its body. *Pomatoschistus minutus*, the **Sand Goby**, grows to larger sizes and has a black patch on the posterior edge of the first dorsal. The **Black Goby** *Gobius niger* is really brown in colour with close-set dorsal fins.

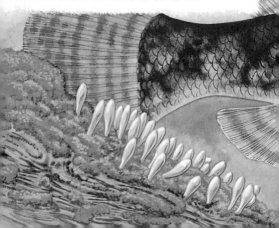

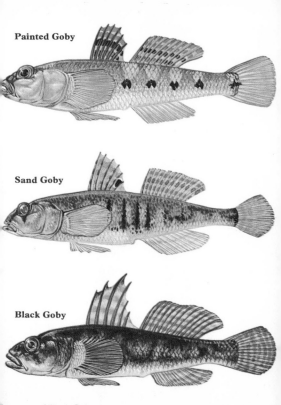

Painted Goby

Sand Goby

Black Goby

Egg cases of Black Goby

195

GREATER SANDEEL
Hyperoplus lanceolatus

A slender Eel-like fish with one long dorsal fin and a
forked tail. Green on the back, the flanks shade to
silver and there is a dark patch at either side of the
fish's elongated snout. Sandeels are shoalfish that
live over offshore sandbanks where they feed on zoo-
plankton. Widely distributed, from the Bay of Biscay
to the arctic North Cape, they are preyed upon by
most of the important food fish and form a major
part of the oceanic life support system.

LESSER SANDEEL *Ammodytes tobianus*

Found in similar habitats, this common species will
bury itself in gently sloping sandy beaches as the
tide recedes. It is often dug up to be used as food or
fisherman's bait.

Head of Greater
Sandeel

Sandbank with Sandeels emerging, swarming with feeding
Bass

Greater Sandeel

LUMPSUCKER *Cyclopterus lumpus*

The Lumpsucker is an awkward fish, aptly named. Found throughout the North Atlantic, it favours

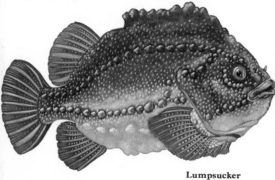

Lumpsucker

rocky ground in shallow areas. The dorsal fin is set far back behind a ridge of bony tubercles. The body is liberally covered in tubercles, the largest being formed into three lateral rows along the flanks. The pelvic fins have become fused to form a suction disc which enables the Lumpsucker to adhere to rocks on the seabed. There is a sexual/colour variation; males are blue-black on the back and sides with a reddish tinge on the underbelly, females have a muted grey-blue coloration. The fish spawn in the spring, after establishing a pair bond, and a huge number of eggs are laid. The male fish guards the eggs until hatched. It is said that the eggs can be used to produce a kind of second-rate caviar.

GUNNEL or BUTTERFISH
Pholis gunnellus

This small-growing species is found throughout the North Atlantic living in shallow waters that offer weed and rocky areas of security. Beloved of small boys, who rake around among the seaweed as the tide recedes, leaving little pools of water or just enough moisture to wet the fish's body, the Butterfish is difficult to pick up – hence its name. It can be

Gunnel

easily recognized by the Eel-shape, with a dorsal fin from head to tail. Its anal fin is half its body length. Generally grey in colour, there are a series of black spots, edged with white, at the base of the dorsal fin.

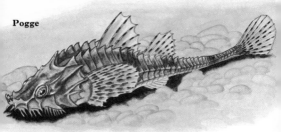

POGGE *Agonus cataphractus*

At first sight the Pogge appears to be a relic from prehistoric times. The fish's body seems to be divided by ridges of armoured plates. There is a group of stiff bristles under the chin and around the mouth. The first dorsal fin is spined and the supporting rays of all fins are speckled with dark brown colouring. This species is demersal; sometimes called the Armed Bullhead, it lives among weedgrowth on soft seabeds.

Wreckfish travel many miles under
floating wreckage

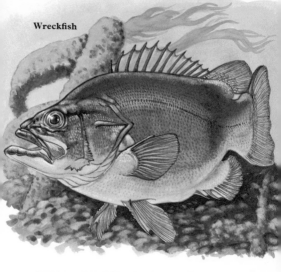

Wreckfish

WRECKFISH *Polyprion americanus*

A large fish, solitary in behaviour, haunting rocky ground in deep water. There is one long dorsal fin. The forward portion has stiff spines, joined with leathery webs, followed by soft rays. The anal fin is short and set far back on the body. There is a prominent bony ridge on each gill case. The colour varies between brown-red and dirty yellow. Wreckfish have extremely small scales for a fish that can weigh over 110 lb (50 kg).

Thin-lipped Mullet

MULLET

Mullet are known as fish of summer. They move
north from the Mediterranean and Iberian Peninsula
to British coastal waters and the shores of France,
Belgium and Holland in late spring. All three species
can be found haunting harbours, where they glide,
almost unseen through the shadows of the boats,
scavenging for titbits among the flotsam. In shallow
estuarine areas, the fish swim with their dorsal fins
cutting the surface film. The **Thin-lipped Mullet**
Liza ramada has a narrow upper lip and a broad
throat slit. **Thick-lipped Mullet** *Crenimugil labrosus* display a thickened upper lip and a very narrow
throat slit. Both species have a distinctive first dorsal
fin with four spined rays. There is no lateral line.

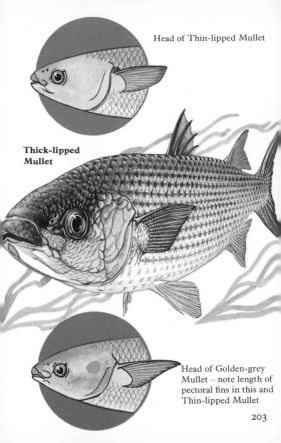

Head of Thin-lipped Mullet

Thick-lipped Mullet

Head of Golden-grey Mullet – note length of pectoral fins in this and Thin-lipped Mullet

GOLDEN-GREY MULLET
Liza auratus

**Distribution map
of Golden-grey Mullet**

Golden-grey Mullet

Less northerly in distribution, this Mullet has a beautiful golden sheen to the scales on its flanks and underbelly. There is a cheek patch of bright yellow. The upper lip is thin and the species exhibits a broad throat slit. In shape, it resembles the grey species. Mullet are important food for the Continent.

SHANNY *Blennius pholis*

An ugly little fish of the rocky coastline, often found in rock pools, where it jealously guards its territory from other small invaders. Behind the broad head, the dorsal extends to the tail with a pronounced cut-out section in the middle. Grey-green coloration is blotched with brown, black and cream. The anal fin has a light edging.

Shanny

HALIBUT *Hippoglossus hippoglossus*

The largest-growing of the 'right-handed' flatfish, it can grow to over 550 lb (250 kg), and is almost arctic in distribution. This powerful, smooth-scaled swimmer is found in deep water off the north-western coasts of Norway, Scotland and Ireland. Halibut live over rocky seabeds and predate voraciously on Cod, Coalfish and other prime species. The body is long and thick with a wide, strong tail ideal for swimming in tide rips and other areas of strong current. Sought-after by commercial long-liners trying to satisfy the demand of European fish markets.

A related species, the **Greenland Halibut** *Reinhardtius hippoglossoides*, has a less symmetrical fin arrangement and an almost straight lateral line. The underside has brown coloration.

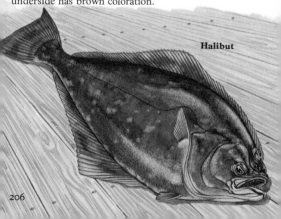

Halibut

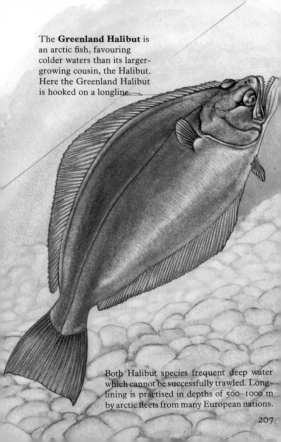

The **Greenland Halibut** is an arctic fish, favouring colder waters than its larger-growing cousin, the Halibut. Here the Greenland Halibut is hooked on a longline.

Both Halibut species frequent deep water which cannot be successfully trawled. Long-lining is practised in depths of 500–1000 m by arctic fleets from many European nations.

Turbot

TURBOT *Scophthalmus maximus*

The largest of the left-handed flatfish, the Turbot is a thick, fleshy, round-shaped species with a broad, powerful tail fin. The upper, coloured side of the fish has a number of bony tubercles extending out to the body margins. The dorsal fin begins just in front of the upper eye and the fish's lateral line takes a pronounced curve over the pectoral fin. Underneath, the Turbot is without scales and nearly pure white in colour. This demersal fish lives over sandbanks and other mixed ground where it feeds largely on live fish, which it catches by ambush as they are swept along in strong currents. The Turbot's mouth is capable of lengthy protrusion, a necessary aid to feeding as the species is not renowned for its swimming speed.

BRILL *Scophthalmus rhombus*

A close relative, smaller-growing, thinner through the body with no tubercles. The skin is covered with minute scales over a mottled grey-brown base coloration. It frequents similar habitats to the Turbot, feeding on small fish and crustaceans.

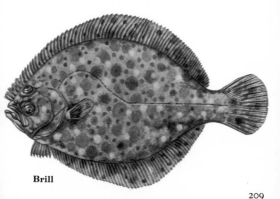

Brill

Megrim

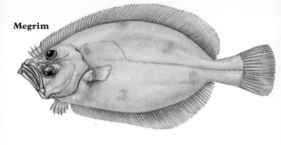

MEGRIM *Lepidorhombus whiffiagonis*

This small flatfish is found in North European waters but rarely in the North Sea, which appears too shallow for the species' life style. A slender, left-handed fish, the body narrows towards the large head with its sizable jaws and eyes. If held up to the light, a Megrim's body is almost transparent. The scales are rough to the touch and easily detached. This fish is quite an important commercial species.

Scaldfish

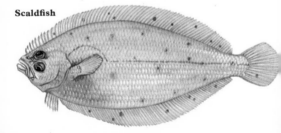

SCALDFISH *Arnoglossus laterna*

Living in deep water over sandy ground, the Scaldfish is a small light brown species with large scales set into skin that is easily torn off – hence the fish's common name. The lateral line is curved over the pectoral fins and the body, with its small mouth and eyes, is Sole-shaped.

Topknot

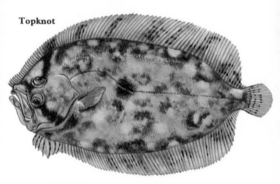

TOPKNOT *Zeugopterus punctatus*

Another small left-handed flatfish with very spiny scales. Almost round in shape, the Topknot appears to be totally surrounded by fins, broken only by the large head and mouth. The species can be found in fairly shallow water over the rough seabed. It is dark brown in colour, with numerous darker blotches.

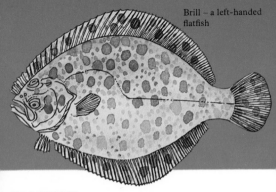

Brill – a left-handed flatfish

FLATFISH:
LEFT AND RIGHT-HANDEDNESS

All flatfish are either left or right-handed. Both eyes are to the right of the mouth in a left-handed fish and to the left of the mouth in a right-handed fish. There are a few exceptions, such as the Flounder which is generally right-handed, although left-handed Flounders are very common – but these fish cannot be regarded as normal.

After hatching from the egg in the upper layers of the sea, all flatfish are symmetrical with an eye on each side of the tiny body. As they grow, feeding on plankton, the body deepens, some blotches of colour appear and one eye migrates around the head to join the other on the coloured side. At this stage in the metamorphosis the flatfish larvae will have descended to begin a benthic, bottom-dwelling

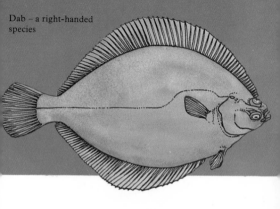
Dab – a right-handed species

existence. The 'blind side' remains colourless in all but a few individuals that may display albinism (white 'coloured' sides) or ambi-coloration (where part of the blind side bears pigmentation).

Left-handed fish:
Bothidae: Scaldfish
Scophthalmidae: Turbot, Brill, Megrim and Topknot.

Right-handed fish:
Pleuronectidae: Halibut, Greenland Halibut, Plaice, Flounder, Dab, Lemon Sole, Long-rough Dab and Witch.

Though not related to other flatfish, the soles are **right-handed:**
Solidae: Dover Sole and Solenette.

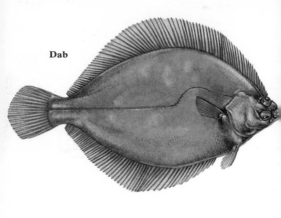

Dab

DAB *Limanda limanda*

The Dab is a widely distributed North European
flatfish, particularly found in shallow areas with a
sandy seabed. It is a slim, right-handed species with
hard scales, especially noticeable when the fish is
rubbed by hand from tail to head. The lateral line is
pronounced and curves sharply over the pectoral fin.
Colour is variable but a mid-brown predominates,
occasionally with lighter blotches. There are no
nodules on the body. Dabs have a thorn at the
beginning of the anal fin.

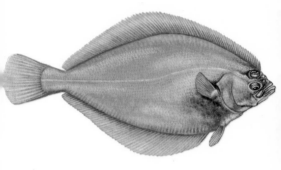

LONG ROUGH DAB
Hippoglossoides platessoides

Unrelated to the Dab, this fish grows larger and is present throughout the North Atlantic temperate and arctic waters. Favouring deeper water it feeds on crustaceans, molluscs and small fish. The scales are large and rough. The lateral line is almost straight and the body has no tubercles. This species is grey-brown in colour, has a large mouth and the dorsal fin begins above the eyes. The Long Rough Dab is not a noted food species as the flesh is flaccid and considered lacking in quality.

215

PLAICE *Pleuronectes platessa*

Found widespread in the North Atlantic, the Plaice is definitely among the most prized of fish both to the sea angler and commercial trawlerman. It lives in sea areas of soft or sandy ground with a wide range of depth: 30–660 ft (10–200 m). Smooth small scales cover its body which has a ridge of bony nodules on the head, behind the eyes. The lateral line is nearly straight, with only a slight curve over the pectorals. Wider in the body than the Dab, Plaice have a spattering of orange spots which spread over both body and fins. The body is less slimy to the touch than the Flounder, which it bears a superficial resemblance to.

Plaice feed on worms, small crustaceans and molluscs, preferring those species with opening shells; mussels are especially popular.

Plaice

FLOUNDER *Platichthys flesus*

This is one flatfish that is tolerant of brackish water, such as estuaries and shallow saltwater lagoons, that have a freshwater inflow. It is often found far up into the Bream zone of lowland rivers. The cold weather of winter drives them downriver, out to the deeper, warmer sea. This species is distributed throughout the European North Atlantic, down and into the Mediterranean Sea. Flounder have a series of bony nodules along the lateral line, beginning behind the fish's gill case. There are more slightly spiny nodules following the line of the base of both dorsal and anal fins. There may be pale orange spots on the body. Although a right-handed fish, over a quarter of a commercial catch may contain left-handed Flounder and many may exhibit colour deviations! Flounder are nocturnal feeders, with an omnivorous diet.

Flounder –
note nodules on
head and body

LEMON SOLE *Microstomus kitt*

An oval-shaped species of northern waters, they live over rocky ground in deep water, feeding on crustaceans, molluscs and invertebrates. The Lemon Sole is an important commercial fish in Britain and on the Continent. Rich brown colouring is marked with greenish-yellow marbling, the body is slimy and the head and mouth noticeably small. Lemon Sole is a name given to a wide range of flatfish by the fish marketing industry, inviting confusion. The **Witch** *Glyptocephalus cynoglossus* is an elongated, deep-water flatfish, spread across the North Atlantic Ocean. It has a small mouth and straight lateral line. The body is a dull brown-grey with rough scales on the coloured side. The blind side is a smoky-white hue. There is a distinct anal thorn.

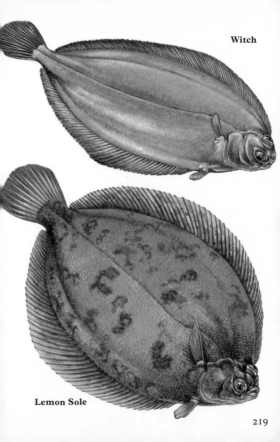

Witch

Lemon Sole

SOLE *Solea solea*

Found around the British Isles, European coast, and into the Mediterranean. This much sought-after species has a distinctive shape, elongate with a blunt rounded head. Two nasal openings are found on the fish's blind side. Brown in colour, there are a number of dark blotches in rows on the body and a black spot at the tip of the pectoral fin. The dorsal fin starts in front of the eyes. Sole are nocturnal feeders on small worms, crustaceans and shellfish. Sometimes called Dover Sole to identify it from the Sand or French

Shore fishing in the evening for Sole

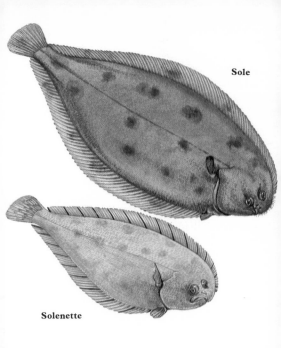

Sole

Solenette

Sole *Pegusa lascaris*. The **Solenette** *Buglossidium luteum* is a tiny flatfish, rarely more than 5 in (12 cm) long. Distribution is similar to the Sole. It is easily recognized by the black rays, distributed evenly through both anal and dorsal fins.

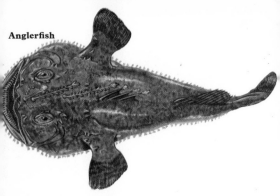

Anglerfish

ANGLERFISH *Lophius piscatorius*

Widespread in North European and Mediterranean waters, this deep-water species is unmistakable in shape and appearance – it seems to be all head! The body is flattened, is bulbous at the head, tapering quickly behind the paddle-like pectoral fins. Its dorsal finning is in four separate divisions: two long, isolated spines in front of the eyes, the first acting as a dangling 'bait' for unwary demersal fish; there follows a single stiff spine, then three spines united by a leathery membrane and, finally, a rayed fin anterior to the tail. The fish's outline is broken up by fringing; fleshy protuberances around the mouth and body held to camouflage the fish as it lies buried in a muddy seabed, waiting to pounce on a variety of other species. The mouth is huge, furnished with two rows of sharp, hinged, curved teeth.

MONKFISH *Squatina squatina*

A most ugly fish of temperate seas, it appears half-Shark and half-Skate, with a flattened body and huge paired fins. The gristly body supports two dorsals, equal in size, and a powerful tail. Grey-brown in colour, there can be spots or streaks of darker hue. The mouth is positioned at the extreme edge of the head unlike the Shark's, to which it is related. It can be found in shallow sandy areas feeding on crabs, shellfish and minor demersal fish. Monkfish disappear in winter to warmer, offshore habitats.

Monkfish

Trout leaping

Phylo-generic Trees

Classification, of the world of Nature, means sorting all animals and plants into groups that have similar characteristics and are best expressed as parts of a tree. The roots go back to the species' ancestral beginnings in geological time. Many of the earlier fish would have been placed on the trunk and main branches of the phylogeneric tree. They are long since extinct – only the outer branches and the smallest twigs represent the modern creature.

The simplest unit of classification is the **species**.

Varieties within a species, such as Mirror Carp, do not constitute a sub or separate species. A number of similar, closely related species come together to form a **genus** (plural **genera**). Individual genera form **families** which are further grouped into **sub-orders** and **orders**. A number of orders will constitute a **sub-class** or **class** which, in turn, join **sub-kingdoms** and **kingdoms**.

Often there will be a name following the scientific (Latin) name. This is the sponsor or discoverer, such as *Linnaeus*, the Swedish naturalist, who would have described the animal for the first time. If that name appears in brackets, it means that the species has since been put into a different genus from that ascribed by the original classifier.

Example   Porbeagle Shark

Species	*Lamna nasus*
Genus	*Lamna*
Family	*Lamnidae*
Order	*Lamniformes*
Sub-Class	*Elasmobranchii*
Class	*Chrondrichthyes*
Sub-Kingdom	*Vertibrata*

Phylogeneric trees according to Gregory.

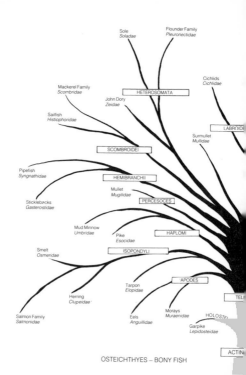

Sole
Soladae

Flounder Family
Pleuronectidae

Cichlids
Cichlidae

HETEROSOMATA

Mackerel Family
Scombridae

John Dory
Zeidae

LABROIDE

Sailfish
Histiophoridae

Surmullet
Mullidae

SCOMBROIDEI

Pipefish
Syngnathidae

HEMIBRANCHII

Mullet
Mugilidae

PERCESOCES

Sticklebacks
Gasterostidae

Mud Minnow
Umbridae

Pike
Esocidae

HAPLOMI

Smelt
Osmenidae

ISOPONDYLI

APODES

Tarpon
Elopidae

TEL

Herring
Clupeidae

Morays
Muraenidae

HOLOSTE

Salmon Family
Salmonidae

Eels
Anguillidae

Garpike
Lepidosteidae

ACTIN

OSTEICHTHYES – BONY FISH

226

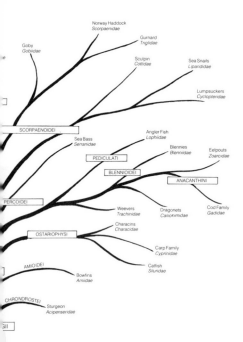

Norway Haddock
Scorpaenidae

Gurnard
Triglidae

Goby
Gobiidae

Sculpin
Cottidae

Sea Snails
Liparidae

Lumpsuckers
Cyclopteridae

SCORPAENOIDEI

Sea Bass
Serranidae

Angler Fish
Lophiidae

Blennies
Blenniidae

Eelpouts
Zoarcidae

PEDICULATI

BLENNIOIDEI

ANACANTHINI

PERCOIDEI

Weevers
Trachinidae

Dragonets
Callionymidae

Cod Family
Gadidae

OSTARIOPHYSI

Characins
Characidae

Carp Family
Cyprinidae

AMIOIDEI

Bowfins
Amiidae

Catfish
Siluridae

CHRONDROSTEI

Sturgeon
Acipenseridae

Gll

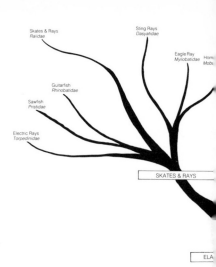

Skates & Rays
Raidae

Sting Rays
Dasyatidae

Eagle Ray
Myliobatidae

Horn
Mobu

Guitarfish
Rhinobatidae

Sawfish
Pristidae

Electric Rays
Torpedinidae

SKATES & RAYS

ELA

CHO

CHONDRICHTHYES – CARTILAGINOUS FISH

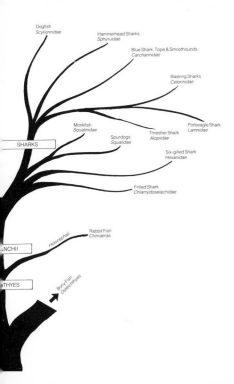

Dogfish
Scylionidae

Hammerhead Sharks
Sphyruidae

Blue Shark, Tope & Smoothhounds
Carcharinidae

Basking Sharks
Cetorinidae

Monkfish
Squatinidae

Spurdogs
Squalidae

Thresher Shark
Alopiidae

Porbeagle Shark
Lamnidae

SHARKS

Six-gilled Shark
Hexanidae

Frilled Shark
Chlamydoselachidae

Rabbit Fish
Chimaeras

Holocephali

NCHII

Bony Fish
Osteichthyes

THYES

Bibliography

Brennan, Desmond, *The Sea Angler: Afloat and Ashore* (1965)

Buller, Fred & Falkus, Hugh, *Freshwater Fishing* (1975)

Couch, Jonathan, *A History of British Fishes* (1877)

Furneaux, W. S., *The Sea Shore* (1903)

Gammon, Clive, *A Tide of Fish* (1962)

Gordon, W. J., *Our Country's Fishes*

Gunther, A. C., *An Introduction to the Study of Fishes* (1880)

Hansen, Jens Ploug, *Adelfisk* (1976)

Hardy, Sir Alister, *The Open Sea* (1956)

Hervey, G. F. & Hems, J., *The Goldfish* (1948)

Houghton, Rev. W., *British Freshwater Fishes* (1879)

Jenkins & Travis, J., *The Fishes of the British Isles* (1936)

Kennedy, Michael, *The Sea Angler's Fishes* (1954)

Magri MacMahon, Prof. A. F., *Fishlore* (1946)

Maitland, Peter S., *Freshwater Fishes of Britain and Europe* (1977)

McClane, A. J., *Standard Fishing Encyclopedia* (1965)

Muus, Bent J., *Collins Guide to the Sea Fishes of Britain and North-West Europe* (1974)

Norman, J. R., *A History of Fishes* (1931)

Prichard, Michael, *Collins Encyclopedia of Fishing* (1977)

Russell, F. S. & Yonge, C. M., *The Seas* (1928)

Wheeler, Alwynne, *The Fishes of the British Isles and North-West Europe* (1969)

Yonge, C. M., *The Sea Shore* (1949)

Index of English names

Entries in italics denote local names

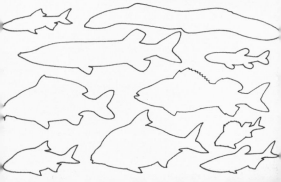

234

235

Perch

Index of Scientific names

Porbeagle Shark